Peter Burian
DSLR α200

Magic Lantern Guides®

SONY®

DSLR

α200

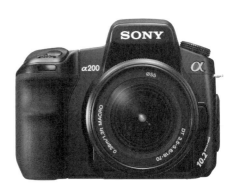

Peter Burian

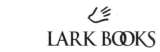

LARK BOOKS

A Division of Sterling Publishing Co., Inc.
New York / London

Book Design and Layout: Michael Robertson
Cover Design: Thom Gaines
Editor: Matt Paden

Library of Congress Cataloging-in-Publication Data
Burian, Peter K.
  Magic lantern guides : SONY DSLR A200 / Peter K. Burian. -- 1st ed.
     p. cm.
  Includes index.
  ISBN-13: 978-1-60059-412-0 (pb-trade pbk. : alk. paper)
  1. Photography--Digital techniques. 2. Single-lens reflex cameras. I.
Title.
  TR267.B856 2008
  771.3'2--dc22

                           2007046182

10 9 8 7 6 5 4 3 2 1
First Edition

Published by Lark Books, A Division of
Sterling Publishing Co., Inc.
387 Park Avenue South, New York, N.Y. 10016

Distributed in Canada by Sterling Publishing,
c/o Canadian Manda Group, 165 Dufferin Street
Toronto, Ontario, Canada M6K 3H6

Distributed in the United Kingdom by GMC Distribution Services,
Castle Place, 166 High Street, Lewes, East Sussex, England BN7 1XU

Distributed in Australia by Capricorn Link (Australia) Pty Ltd.,
P.O. Box 704, Windsor, NSW 2756 Australia

If you have questions or comments about this book, please contact:
Lark Books
67 Broadway
Asheville, NC 28801
(828) 253-0467

Manufactured in the USA

ISBN 13: 978-1-60059-412-0

For information about custom editions, special sales, premium and corporate purchases, please contact Sterling Special Sales Department at 800-805-5489 or specialsales@sterlingpub.com.

Contents

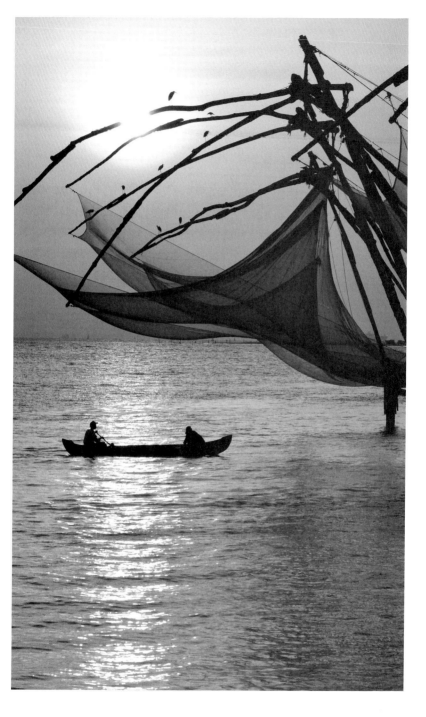

Understanding Digital Photography

The Sony-Konica Minolta Connection

In July 2005, Konica Minolta and Sony issued a press release indicating an agreement to jointly develop digital SLR cameras using technology to be provided by both companies. Then, in January 2006, Konica Minolta announced that it would withdraw from the photo products market and transfer some of its assets to Sony. Subsequently, Sony developed its own digital single lens reflex (D-SLR) cameras employing the most valuable features from the Maxxum/Dynax D-SLRs plus sophisticated Sony technology, as well as some new amenities.

By 2007, Sony was marketing two models, the entry-level ∝100 and the high-end ∝700, covered in other Magic Lantern Guides. In January 2008 at the Consumer Electronics Show, the company unveiled the replacement for the ∝100. The ∝200 includes some new features and technology for 1.7x faster autofocus, better image quality, greater convenience and ease of operation.

The ∝200 is compatible with all Sony accessories and lenses (including the Carl Zeiss Alpha series). You will also find you can use most Maxxum/Dynax lenses and accessories. For those familiar with Konica-Minolta's Anti-Shake system, the ∝200 body includes an improved compensating system for camera shake now called Super SteadyShot (SSS). It's also equipped with Sony's system designed to prevent dust from accumulating on the sensor of this camera.

☜ *While the ∝200 is useful for quick snap shooting with great simplicity, this camera also holds the potential for serious photography, offering the best of both worlds. Its improved technology will also help to satisfy the photo enthusiast who wants faster speed, better image quality, and greater operating convenience.*

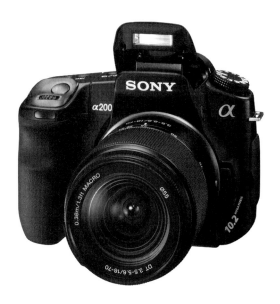

Differences Between Digital and Film Photography

Not very long ago it was easy to tell the difference between photos taken with a digital camera and those shot with a traditional film camera: Pictures from digital cameras didn't have the same quality as those from film. However, this is no longer true. With the ∝200, you can make 13 x 19-inch (33 x 48 cm) prints that look as good, or better, than an enlargement from a 35mm negative. When made from your technically best images, even larger prints can be suitable for framing.

Whether digital or film-based, a camera is basically a light-tight box that holds a lens to focus the image. You regulate the amount of light entering this box to strike the light-sensitive medium (film or sensor) by adjusting the f/stop or the shutter speed. However, in traditional photography the image is recorded on film and later developed with chemicals, while in digital photography the camera converts the light to an electronic image. A digital camera immediately processes this image internally and stores it temporarily on a memory card for downloading, while a film camera stores the exposed film for processing at a later time. While many exposure techniques remain the same, digital photography will help you take advantage of a number of enjoyable and creative possibilities available with this new technology.

The Digital Sensor vs. Film

Both film and digital cameras expose pictures in nearly identical fashion. The light measuring (metering) methods are the same, both work with ISO-based systems, and the shutter and aperture mechanisms controlling the amount of light admitted into the camera are the same. These similarities exist because both film and digital cameras share the same goal: to deliver the appropriate amount of light required by the film or sensor to create a good picture.

Not surprisingly, however, digital sensors respond differently to light than film does. From dark areas (such as navy blue blazers, asphalt, and shadows) to mid-tones (blue sky and green grass) to bright areas (such as white houses and sand beaches), a digital sensor responds to the full range of light equally, or linearly. Film, however, responds linearly only to mid-tones (those blue skies and green fairways). Therefore, negative film blends tones very well in highlight areas and slide film blends tones well in shadow areas, whereas digital sensors often cut out the bright tones. Digital responds to highlights like slide film and to shadows like negative film.

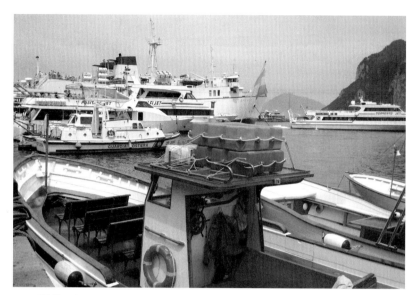

While photographic film was a very useful medium for image capture, a digital sensor and processor provide several significant advantages, including the ability to switch the ISO (sensitivity) on demand. This is particularly useful in situations where you will shoot both indoors and out or when the light level is changing rapidly.

Memory Cards vs. Film

Memory cards are necessary to store images captured by a digital camera. These removable, reusable cards offer several advantages over film:

More Photos/More ISOs: Standard 35mm film cassettes are available in either 24 or 36 exposures. Memory cards come in a wide range of capacities, and all but the smallest are capable of holding more exposures than a roll of film (depending on the selected file size). Also, a single card can record different ISO settings on a picture-by-picture basis—much simpler than switching rolls of film.

Reusable: Once you make an exposure with film, the emulsion layer is permanently changed and the film cannot be reused. With a memory card, you can erase photos at any time, removing the ones you don't want, and creating space for additional photos. This simplifies the process of dealing with and organizing your final set of images. Once images are transferred to your computer (or other storage medium, such as a CD or DVD), images can be erased or the card can be reformatted and reused.

Durability: Memory cards are much more durable than film. They can be removed from the camera in virtually any conditions without the risk of ruined pictures. They are less susceptible to heat damage and can even be taken through the airport carry-on x-ray inspection machines without suffering damage. (However, the cards are susceptible to magnetic fields, so keep them away from stereo speakers and other devices containing powerful magnets.)

Small Size: In the space taken up by just a couple of rolls of film, you can store or tote multiple memory cards that will hold hundreds, if not thousands, of images.

Greater Image Permanence: The latent image (exposed but undeveloped film) is susceptible to degradation from atmospheric conditions such as heat and humidity. And new security monitors for packed and carry-on luggage can also damage film. Traveling photographers find that digital photography allows them much more peace of mind. Not only are memory cards more durable, but their images can also be easily downloaded into storage devices or laptops. No more concerns over what to do with precious exposed film!

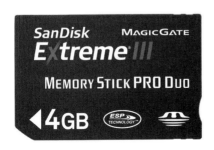

With an optional adapter, the A200 can accept the Pro Duo cards; this is ideal for those who already own such media.

The A200 was primarily designed to be used with CompactFlash cards, including Sony's own series of ultra-fast 300x media.

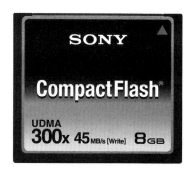

The LCD Monitor

In conventional photography, you are never really sure your picture is a success until the film is developed. You must wait to find out if the exposure was correct or if something happened to spoil the results, such as the blurring of a moving subject or unwanted stray reflections from an on-camera flash.

When using a D-SLR, however, you can see an image on the LCD monitor almost immediately after taking a picture. Admittedly, you cannot see all the details that you would see in a print, but this ability means that you can evaluate the picture you have just shot. If the exposure, lighting, or composition is not quite right, simply re-shoot on the spot. This feature is especially useful in flash photography. In addition to confirming correct exposure, the LCD monitor allows you to check for any excessively bright highlight areas or dark

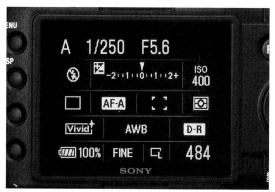

Aside from displaying pictures in Auto Review and Playback modes, the LCD is also used for navigating menus and showing information.

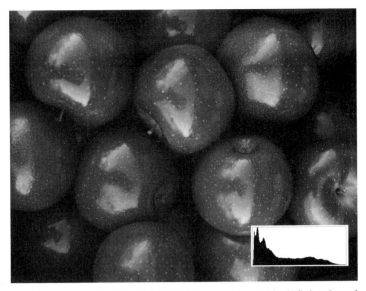

A histogram depicts the distribution of tones from black (left edge of graph) to white (right edge of graph). This histogram is weighted toward dark tones because it corresponds to a low key photo of red apples in shadow with only a small amount of highlight. © Kevin Kopp

backgrounds, as well as allowing you to evaluate other factors, such as the effect produced by multiple flash units and/or reflectors.

Exposure and the Histogram

Digital cameras do not offer magic tricks that let you beat the laws of physics, so incorrect exposure will still cause problems. Too little light makes dark images; too much light makes overly bright images. Granted, you can correct digital images to a certain extent afterwards by using software in a computer, but programs can't create blown details that don't exist in overexposed images. Getting the correct exposure in-camera can save you a great deal of post-processing work.

After you shoot a digital image, a quick glance at the LCD monitor will indicate whether the exposure (image brightness) is close to accurate. Better yet, you can also access a feature that provides a more scientific evaluation of brightness values: the histogram scales (see page 136 for details). Because you are able to check exposure using these scales, there is less need to bracket (shoot a series of images at different exposure levels) when using the ∝200 than with a traditional film camera.

ISO (Sensitivity)

Digital sensors don't have a true ISO. However, their sensitivity has been adjusted electronically to mimic film ISOs. Hence, you can set the ISO to 100 for average daylight shooting, 800 for faster shutter speeds, or smaller apertures in less bright situations, or 1600—and even ISO 3200—for lowlight photography. With a digital camera, you can change ISO from picture to picture, without changing memory cards. It's like changing film at the touch of a button! This provides certain benefits, such as the ability to first shoot indoors without flash at ISO 800, then follow your subject outside into bright sun and optimize image quality by switching immediately to ISO 100.

Noise/Grain

Grain in film appears as an irregular, sand-like texture that, if large, can be unsightly and, if small, is essentially invisible. (A textured look is sometimes desirable for certain creative effects.) It occurs due to the chemical structure of the light sensitive materials and is most prominent in fast films, such as ISO 1600.

The equivalent of grain in digital photography is known as noise, which often occurs as colored specks most visible in dark or evenly-colored mid-tone areas. Digital noise occurs for several reasons: sensor noise (caused by heat from the electronics and optics), digital artifacts (when digital technology cannot deal with fine tonalities such as sky gradations), and JPEG artifacts (caused by image compression). Sensor noise is the most common.

Although the ∝200 provides extra noise reduction processing at ISO 1600 to 3200, digital noise is most prominent in images made at high ISO settings (especially at ISO 1600 or higher), and will increase as the ISO increases.

The mottled colored specks are even more obvious in images that are underexposed and lightened afterward in image processing software. You can buy aftermarket software for further noise reduction, but it's best to use ISO 400 or lower whenever practical for the absolutely "cleanest" images.

Sensor noise may also be increased with long exposures under low-light conditions, as in night photography. However, the camera's long exposure noise reduction feature is automatically activated for exposures of one second or longer; additional processing is applied to minimize the digital noise pattern. In most situations, the ∝200 produces images with very little digital noise at ISO settings up to 800 and acceptable digital noise at ISO 1600.

File Formats

A digital camera converts analog image information to digital data and records to a digital file. The ∝200 offers two distinct file formats: JPEG and RAW. It also offers another option: RAW + JPEG, which records each photo in both the RAW and the JPEG (Fine quality and Large size) formats simultaneously.

JPEG: An acronym for Joint Photographic Experts Group, JPEG is the most common format in digital photography, and is actually a standard for compression of images rather than a true file format. Digital cameras use JPEG because its compression reduces file size, allowing more pictures to fit on a memory card.

RAW: A generic term for a format that has little or no internal processing applied by the camera. Most camera manufacturers have developed proprietary versions of RAW, and the ∝200's RAW files are noted by the suffix "ARW" (but I will often refer to ARW files with the generic term RAW).

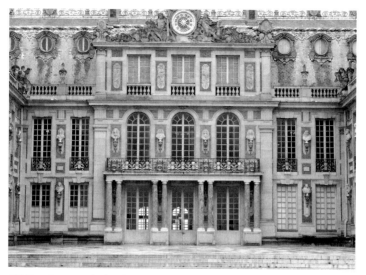

While a low resolution image looks great on a computer monitor, and perhaps in a small print, high resolution is definitely preferable for other purposes. The A200 provides various resolution level options that you can select, but usually you'll want to take advantage of the camera's full 10MP potential.

Resolution

Resolution refers to the quantity of pixels being utilized. Virtually all of today's digital cameras give you choices about how many of the sensor's pixels to use when shooting pictures. You do not always need to employ the camera's maximum resolution. Your memory card will hold more images when the camera is set to record at lower resolutions, but it will not capture as much data; and the more digital information (higher resolution), the bigger the print it is possible to make.

White Balance

Most pros who have shot film over the years can tell you about the challenges of balancing their light source with the film's response to the color of light. For example, daylight-balanced (outdoor) film used indoors under tungsten household lamps will produce pictures with an orange cast. Accurate color reproduction in this instance would require the use of a blue color-correction filter.

The color of light also varies in other circumstances, though our eyes and brain make natural adjustments so we do not notice this variation. Light is quite blue on an overcast day, even bluer in a shady area, green under fluorescent lighting, orange under tungsten lamps, and so on. In film photography, filters attached to the front of a lens can correct for the color cast by altering the color of the light so our subjects are rendered as we normally see them.

This has changed with digital cameras. Color correction is managed by the built-in white balance functions. The camera can automatically check the light, calculate the proper setting for its color temperature, and make the necessary modification. This automated system is programmed to produce pictures without color casts or inaccurate tones. However, this system is not foolproof, so user-selectable white balance overrides are also usually provided.

Cost of Shooting

While film cameras generally cost less than digital cameras, the cost of shooting digital is lower. A couple of reusable memory cards are much less expensive than a large supply of film, and there's no need to pay for processing or for printing every image on a roll of film. The more pictures you take, the sooner you will recoup the difference in the cost of an ∝200 versus the cost of a comparable 35mm film camera.

More importantly perhaps, you may become a better photographer when using a digital camera. Since you won't need to worry about the cost of film and processing, you'll be more likely to really "work" a subject, exploring it from various angles and trying a variety of creative photographic approaches. This can be liberating because it encourages greater creativity. Any shots that don't work out can simply be deleted.

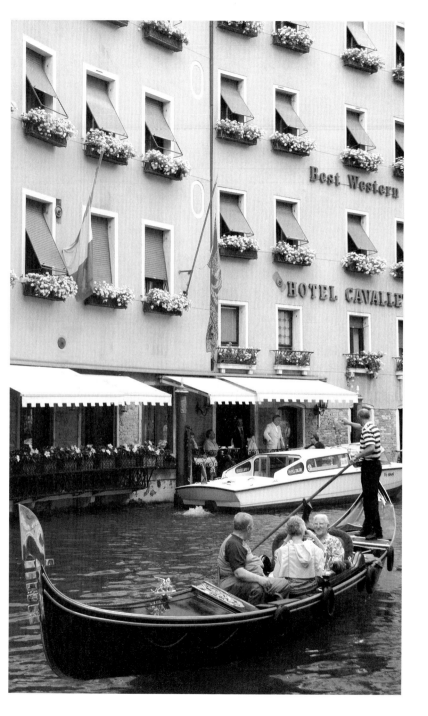

Features and Functions

Although this is a very affordable entry-level D-SLR, the ∝200 is a versatile model and possesses some technology not available in other cameras in the same class. While it's easy to use for those new to digital SLRs, the ∝200 will also satisfy some experienced photographers thanks to its many advanced capabilities.

This compact D-SLR features a large rubberized handgrip as well as sizeable, easy-to-manipulate external controls. It's finished with a scratch-resistant matte black exterior over a strong metal chassis. Its high-resolution, 2.7-inch (6.2 cm) color LCD monitor with a wide viewing angle is adequately large for convenient image viewing. This screen features an anti-reflection coating to make the display more visible in sunny outdoor locations.

The screen is used for menu navigation and for displaying data about current camera settings in large, easy-to-read text. It also displays recorded images after they are taken. In after-shot viewing or in Playback mode, full shooting data—plus a histogram display—is available for each image. The display's orientation automatically switches from landscape to portrait position when the camera is turned on its side.

The ∝200 is designed with fewer control buttons than some entry-level cameras, so it's less likely to intimidate a first time D-SLR user. However, it allows for many features to be selected quickly, using the large Mode dial on the cam-era's left shoulder and the Function **Fn** button on the back. The latter activates a sub-menu that includes only fre-

↻ *The Sony DSLR-∝200 offers advantages over less sophisticated point-and-shoot digital cameras, including a larger image sensor (for better quality), faster response time and framing rate, as well as compatibility with a wide range of lenses, from macro to wide angle and telephoto.*

23

quently-used features. A range of additional functions is accessed using other buttons and various menus discussed in detail later in this chapter.

This is an autofocus camera, but it allows for manual focus, using the pertinent ring on any lens, when the AF/MF switch (on the front) is set to MF.

The camera features the Alpha lens mount, identical to the Konica Minolta Maxxum/Dynax A mount. Although it is not compatible with Minolta manual focus lenses (MD and MC), the camera accepts Maxxum/Dynax AF lenses made since 1985. While Sony does not guarantee that all such lenses are completely compatible, we doubt there will be many, if any, compatibility problems. Naturally, all Sony brand G-series AF lenses—and the Carl Zeiss ZA (Zeiss Alpha) series made specifically for the Sony an A system— are fully compatible. Like some of the Maxxum/Dynax lenses, an increasing number of Sony and ZA lenses incorporate the SSM (Super Sonic Wave) focus motor, employing ultrasonic drive technology.

The ∝200 also features Sony's latest BIONZ processing engine to provide images with maximum detail, accurate colors, and minimal digital noise. It's very fast and allows you to fill your memory card while shooting numerous JPEGs at 3 frames per second (fps). Even after taking a long burst of photos, the camera is usually ready for more shots. To derive maximum speed performance, use a high-speed CompactFlash card: 133x, 233x, or an even faster Sony 300x card.

A unique D-Range Optimizer (DRO) feature is made possible by the BIONZ engine. Three options are available: Off, Standard **D-R** , and Advanced **D-R+** . The Optimizer makes gamma and tone adjustments for technically better images. According to Sony, "DRO assures perfectly exposed pictures, especially when shooting high-contrast or strongly backlit scenes that can lead to loss of highlight and shadow detail."

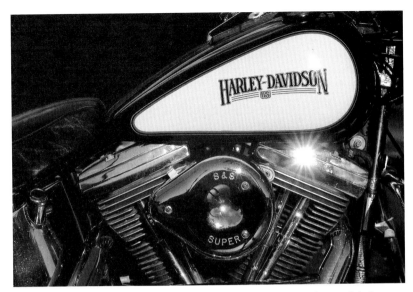

The Dynamic Range Optimizer feature is particularly useful for scenes of high contrast, helping to provide a technically better image.

The camera also features Eye-start, a system with two sensors located just below the viewfinder eyepiece (with its rubber cup). These detect the presence of the user as he or she places their face to the viewfinder; that automatically starts the light metering and autofocus systems so the camera will be ready to shoot immediately. After that detection occurs, the LCD monitor is dimmed to conserve battery power.

Spend time with your ∝200, getting to know it well. Become familiar with each of the controls. Many of the abbreviations and icons used to denote the various features are common to other digital cameras, so they may already be familiar. Some are intuitive; for example, WB stands for white balance, AF/MF denotes autofocus/manual focus, AEL stands for auto exposure lock, and so on.

Sony α200 – Topview

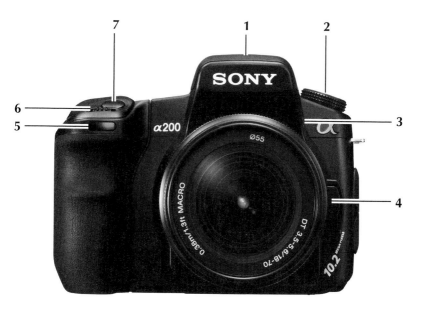

1. Built in flash
2. Mode dial
3. Flash pop up button
4. Lens release button
5. Self timer lamp
6. Control dial
7. Shutter button

Sony ∝200 – Backview

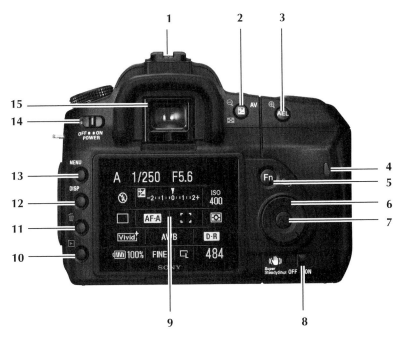

1. Hot shoe
2. Exposure button / Zoom out button
3. Auto exposure lock / Zoom in button
4. Access lamp
5. Function button / Image rotation button
6. Controller
7. Controller (Enter) / Spot AF button
8. Super SteadyShot switch
9. LCD monitor
10. Playback button
11. Delete button
12. DISP (Display) button / LCD brightness button
13. MENU button
14. Power switch
15. Viewfinder

Sony ∝200 – Topview

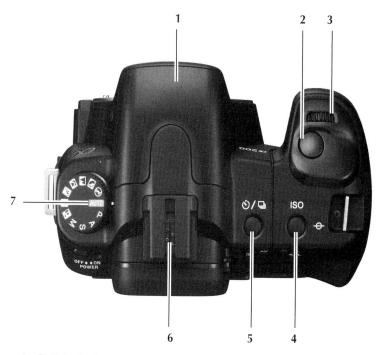

1. Built-in flash
2. Shutter button
3. Control dial
4. ISO button

5. Drive buttom
6. Hot shoe
7. Mode dial

Overview of Features

Though compact, the ∝200 is a full-featured camera with many automatic, semi-automatic, and manual options. It is easy to use in point-and-shoot modes, but is highly suitable for serious photography due to its versatility.

- A 10MP (effective) sensor with 3,872 x 2,592 pixel resolution, developed by Sony.
- A 2.7-inch (6.2 cm) LCD monitor provides provides high resolution (230,000 pixels) for a clear, crisp display. It also possesses a wide viewing angle and anti-reflection coating to resist the effects of glare.
- The Eye-Start system quickly activates all camera systems, including autofocus, before depressing the shutter button.
- An improved version of the sophisticated BIONZ Image Processing Engine maximizes detail and color integrity and minimizes digital noise.
- The Super SteadyShot (SSS) system compensates for camera shake. This in-camera CCD-Shift system stabilizes most Maxxum/Dynax and all Sony or Carl Zeiss ZA (Zeiss Alpha) lenses, providing an advantage of 2–3.5 increments of shutter speed over non-stabilized cameras/lenses.
- A D-Range Optimizer that makes brightness and tone adjustments in high-contrast lighting conditions—especially back lighting. In practical terms, the system provides increased shadow detail and better highlight detail under high-contrast lighting.
- An Anti-Dust system to shake loose dust particles from the sensor whenever the camera is turned off. The ∝200 is also equipped with special anti-static coating on the low-pass filter to minimize static electricity and dust attraction.
- A new rechargeable battery that is rated to provide 750 shots on a single charge, assuming 50% flash usage (CIPA standard). This InfoLithium battery allows the camera to provide data about percentage of battery life remaining.

Specifications

Image Sensor: 23.6 x 15.8 mm CCD with RGB filter array and low-pass filter; 10.2 million recording pixels; 1.5x field of view crop.

Image Size: L: 10MP; M: 5.6MP; S: 2.5MP.

Quality: JPEG Fine and JPEG Standard; RAW (ARW format); and RAW+JPEG options.

Sensitivity: ISO 100 to 3200; also, Auto ISO selection.

Viewfinder: Penta-mirror finder, 95% field of view; 0.83x magnification; Spherical Acute Matte focusing screen; diopter correction, -2.5 to +1; removable eyepiece cup; eye relief of 17.6mm (from eye-piece).

Shutter Speeds: 30 to 1/4000 sec. plus Bulb; top flash sync speed 1/160 or 1/125 when Super SteadyShot is active.

Exposure Modes: AUTO, Program (shiftable), Aperture and Shutter Priority AE, Manual, plus seven scene modes.

Drive: Single frame and Continuous at up to 3 fps advance; Self-timer.

Autofocus System: Nine-point sensor with cross hatched central point; any sensor selectable; Single shot AF, Continuous predictive tracking AF and auto switching between AF modes; focus override in AF mode available; focus-assist beam with pre-flash; Eye-Start AF system.

Exposure Metering: Center weighted; Spot; 40-segment honeycomb pattern (evaluative); exposure and flash exposure compensation; AE Lock and AE bracketing for ambient light and/or flash.

White Balance: Automatic, Daylight, Shade, Cloudy, Tungsten, Fluorescent, Flash, and Custom WB; White balance fine tuning and bracketing; Color Temperature (2500-9900K) also selectable.

Creative Styles: Standard, Vivid, Portrait, Landscape, Sunset, Night View, and B&W in sRGB color space; also, Adobe RGB selectable; contrast, color saturation, and sharpness adjustment level options.

Noise Reduction: High ISO and Long Exposure Noise reduction with On/Off control.

Flash: Built-in, with automatic pop-up in some exposure modes and manual "up" control; pre-flash TTL; also, ADI metering with Maxxum D-series and Sony or Carl Zeiss ZA lenses; Fill-flash, Flash cancel, Slow Sync, and Rear Curtain Sync modes; Flash Exposure Bracketing and Compensation available; wireless off-camera TTL flash and high-speed sync available with certain flash units.

Power: One NP-FM500H Lithium-Ion rechargeable battery (1600 mAh); optional AC adapter; also, optional battery pack/vertical grip VG-B30AM for use with one or two NP-FM500H batteries.

Connectivity: USB 2.0 High-speed; Video out (NTSC or PAL); DC-in AC adapter; socket for remote control accessory.

Dimensions/Weight: 5.25 x 42.8 inches; 18.8 oz. without battery; (130.8 x 98.5 x 71.3mm; 532g).

Software Supplied: Image Data Lightbox SR 2.0 and Image Data Lightbox for Windows and Mac; also, Picture Motion Browser for Windows. (This may vary by geographic location.)

Other Features: Orientation sensor for LCD data and images; USB 2.0 High-speed output; accepts CompactFlash I and II cards and, with adapter, Memory Stick Duo or PRO Duo cards.

Optional Accessories: Compatible with Maxxum/Dynax D-series flash units and Sony HVL flash units; also with certain other Konica Minolta flash units with optional adapter; accepts Sony Alpha series accessories plus a wide range of Maxxum/Dynax accessories.

Camera Activation

Power Switch

The main power switch is located on back of the camera in the upper left corner. This switch slides right to turn ON and left to turn OFF.

Power Save

The ∝200 will basically shut down if it is on but has not been operated for a given length of time (the default is one minute). This is known as Power save and is meant to save battery power. Simply press the shutter button to reactivate the camera so it is ready to shoot.

You can use [Setup menu 1 ⚒ 1] to vary the length of inoperative time before the camera will automatically begin Power save mode. See page 95 for details.

External Ports

The camera features several terminals for attaching acces-sories. On the left side, you will find a port for the optional AC Adapter AC-VQ900AM and the remote con-trol terminal. The optional remote cords RM-S1AM and the longer RM-L1AM can be used to remotely trigger the shutter, which helps to eliminate camera vibration during long exposures.

On the right side of the camera body you will find a door covering the memory card slot and the USB port/Video Out terminal. The USB cable included in the ∝200 camera kit connects the camera to a computer's USB port for down-loading image files, or to some recent PictBridge compatible printers for printing directly from the camera (see pages 201-

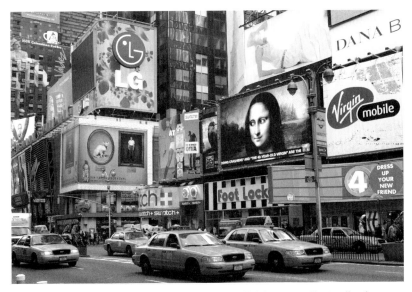

Virtually all photo printers today are PictBridge compliant, allowing for direct printing from the camera when connected with a USB cable. Most printer manufacturers now market compact portable printers that can be used to make prints quickly, without a computer, while traveling or enjoying a family celebration.

203 for more information). The camera also accepts the second cable included in the kit. This is used for connecting the camera to a television monitor's video-in port for showing images on a large screen.

Resetting Controls

Once you become familiar with your ∝200 you are likely to change settings often. Sometimes you may want to quickly return to the original default settings. To do so, use the [Reset] option in [Recording menu 2 ◘ 2] (see page 87 for details) and [Reset Default] in [Setup Menu 3 ◥ 3] (see page 99 for details).

Camera Controls

There are several important controls on the ∝200 that are used to navigate and manage camera functions. (Other buttons are also available and these, and their functions, will be discussed in subsequent chapters.)

The Mode Dial
Located on the camera's top left shoulder, this dial is used for selecting the exposure mode. The abbreviations P, A, S, and M denote Program mode (shiftable, so you can change the aperture/shutter speed combination), Aperture Priority, Shutter Priority (both semi-automatic), and Manual (for manual selection of both aperture and shutter speed using guidance from the camera's light meter, but without automation.)

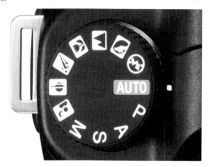

AUTO denotes fully automatic (no aperture/shutter speed shift available), while the picture icons denote Portrait 🐾 , Landscape 🏔 , Macro (close-up) 🌷 , Sports Action 🏃 , Sunset ☀ , and Night View/Portrait 🌃 . Auto with Flash off 🚫⚡ is also available to prevent automatic flash pop-up in a fully automatic mode. Each was designed to produce good photos with the specific type of scene or subject.

Controller
This circular pad on the back of the camera has arrow keys that allow you to scroll up, down, right, and left. The button in the center of the pad is often used as an "Enter" button to

confirm a selection in the electronic menu or in the Function sub-menu. It's marked AF because it has another function: setting Spot AF area, discussed in chapter 5.

Function 🅵🅽 Button

Located above the Controller, this button activates a sub-menu for access to specific functions and the options for each of them. Use it to access [Flash mode], [Autofocus mode], [White Balance], [Metering Mode], [AF Area], and [D-Range Optimizer]. Scroll to the desired item with the Controller and press the central AF button when you reach the one you want. That will activate the list of options available for that item; scroll to the one you want and press the central AF button again to enter and confirm your selection.

Power Sources

The single proprietary rechargeable Sony Lithium-Ion (Li-Ion) battery (NP-FM500H, included with the camera) will power about 750 frames per charge, though you'll get fewer shots if you frequently use the built-in flash or the image playback feature. The number of shots per charge is also dependent on the external temperature; if bitter cold outside, the battery will drain more quickly. When the camera is on, the data in the LCD screen (lower left corner) provides an indication, in percent, of the remaining battery capacity, thanks to the new InfoLithium feature. Maximum recharging time for a dead battery is about 175 minutes for a Normal Charge or 235 minutes for a Full Charge.

The ∝200 does not accept universally available batteries, such as AAs, so it is wise to carry a spare NP-FM500H, especially on long outings. If you buy the optional battery pack/vertical grip VG-B30AM, you can insert two of the batteries into this accessory; the camera will use one first and switch to the second one as necessary.

Sony ∝200 – Viewfinder

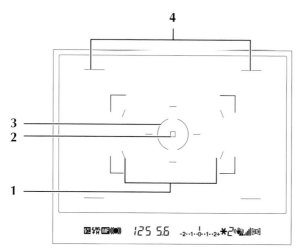

1. AF area
2. Spot AF area

3. Spot metering area
4. Shooting area for 16:9 aspect ratio

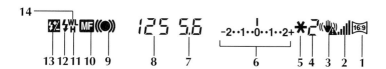

1. Aspect ratio
2. Super Steady Shot scale
3. Camera-shake warning
4. Shots-remaining counter
5. AE lock
6. EV scale
7. Aperture
8. Shutter speed

9. Focus
10. Manual focus
11. High-speed sync
12. Flash (Blinking=charging, lit=charged)
13. Flash compensation
14. Wireless flash

The camera can also be plugged into household power using the optional AC adapter (be sure to use the correct power cord for your geographic region). This option is useful for preventing battery drain if you download images directly from the camera to a computer, or plan to print directly from the camera while it's connected to a printer with a USB cable.

The Viewfinder

The α200 uses an eye-level viewfinder with a Spherical Acute Matte focusing screen and a large, bright, lightweight, and specially coated penta-mirror (instead of the heavier, all-glass pentaprism that is used in some cameras). The finder shows 95% of the image area at 0.83x magnification when using a 50mm lens focused at infinity. That level of magnification is about average in the affordable D-SLR category. The eyepoint is 17.6 mm, indicating that you can see the entire image area when holding the camera—without the rubber eyepiece cup—as far as 20 mm from your eye. (When the eyepiece cup is on the camera, the eye relief is 13.5 mm.) This is beneficial for those who wear eyeglasses when shooting, and are unable to hold the eyepiece closer to their eyes.

The viewfinder eyepiece allows for a -2.5 to +1 diopter adjustment. Adjustments are made using the small diopter adjustment dial on the right side of the rubber eyepiece cup on the back of the camera. If you normally wear eyeglasses, try this feature to determine whether it's adequate to allow you to shoot effectively without your corrective lenses. If not, then make the adjustment while wearing your eyeglasses or ask your retailer about the optional Sony Eyepiece Correctors, which offer higher strengths than those built into the camera.

The viewfinder includes a data display panel (at the bottom of the screen) with information about camera settings in use. Nine AF area points and the spot metering circle are etched on the viewfinder's ground glass screen. When using the camera in autofocus, one or more of the AF area points light up briefly to indicate the point of focus.

When you are using a long shutter speed, a Camera Shake Warning Indicator (📳) is automatically activated at the right end of the data panel in the viewfinder; when this appears, blurring from camera shake is likely. Turn the camera's Super SteadyShot (stabilizer) system On, with the ((📳)) control, and a shake scale ▄▄▌▌ appears in the data panel. This indicates the extent of camera shake compensation that the system is providing at any time. The more bars that appear, the more aggressively the system is working. When five bars appear—and especially when the (📳) is visible—the system may not be fully successful in correcting camera shake; select a higher ISO for a faster shutter speed or brace the camera (or your elbows) on a firm support.

The LCD Monitor

The ∝200 employs a single, full color LCD "Clear Photo" screen on the back of the camera that displays shooting data as well as images (after they are taken). This large LCD is a high resolution screen (230,400 pixels) covered with an anti-reflective coating that helps you view the monitor even in bright conditions when glare would otherwise be a more serious problem. The LCD not only displays important recording data and camera settings, it lets you review pictures stored on your memory card as well as navigate within the full menu and Function sub-menu to control many of the camera's operations.

In order to save battery power, the LCD automatically darkens after a period of non-use. (The default is five seconds, but the time period can be adjusted in [Setup Menu 1 🔧 1], using the [Info Display Time] item; see page 95.) Touching any button or turning any dial or knob quickly re-activates the monitor because the information is always live on the screen whenever the camera's systems are active. Only its backlight automatically switches off to save power.

Sony A200 – LCD Monitor

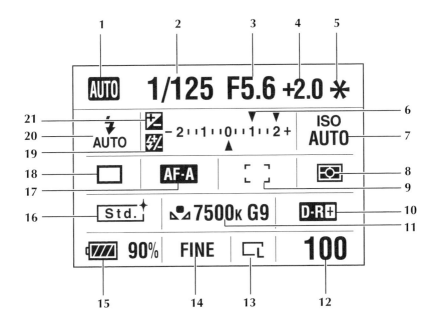

1. Mode dial
2. Shutter speed
3. Aperture
4. Exposure
5. AE lock
6. EV scale
7. ISO sensitivity
8. Metering
9. AF area
10. D Range Optimizer
11. White balance
12. Remaining image number on card
13. Image size
14. Image quality
15. Battery life remaining
16. Creative style
17. Focus mode
18. Drive mode
19. Flash compensation
20. Flash mode
21. Exposure compensation / Metered manual

39

You cannot use the LCD monitor for composing or viewing your picture before shooting, as you can with the more expensive Sony ∝300 and ∝350 cameras. However, the monitor does display an image for quick review immediately after shooting; this feature is called Auto Review by Sony, but photographers often call it instant playback. You can set the length of time you want the [Auto Review] image to be visible before the LCD screen returns to data display in [Custom Menu 1 ✿1] (see page 90). Or you can examine recorded images from your memory card at any time for as long as you want by pressing the Playback button ▶ (back of camera in lower left corner).

By default, the LCD monitor automatically turns off when you hold the camera to your eye; this is achieved through the use of the eye detector sensor under the viewfinder's eyepiece. This conserves power and eliminates the distraction of seeing the display while shooting. When you move the camera away from the shooting position, the data display switches back on automatically. You can deactivate this feature by selecting [Off] for the [Auto off w/VF] item in [Custom menu 1 ✿1], but I do not recommend doing so.

Data Display
Data is displayed on the LCD monitor when images or menus are not being viewed. By default, the LCD screen displays only a few items of data, in large type. If you want to see more data, press the DISP button on the back of the camera; additional items will now appear—in full data display—though in smaller type. When the ∝200 is placed in the vertical shooting position, the display automatically rotates for ease of viewing.

While the camera is in the Recording mode, the expanded display provides a wide scope of useful information on settings and camera operations, ranging from readouts telling which exposure mode and f/stop are in use to remaining battery power and the number of frames left on your memory card. You can scroll between the full and partial display of recording information (or turn the monitor off) by repeatedly pressing the DISP button.

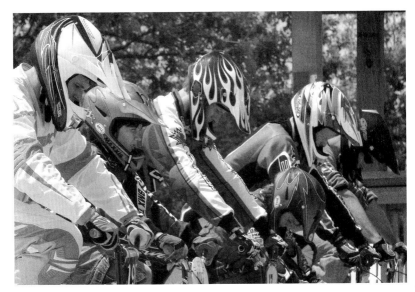

The Auto Review feature is useful when you want to quickly confirm that the photo is technically acceptable. When you want to evaluate an image for a longer time, use the Playback mode.

Note: When the LCD monitor is turned off, neither data nor images can be displayed.

Playback Options

Auto Review (instant playback) occurs automatically after you take a photo. The default viewing period is five seconds, which can be changed in [Custom Menu 1 ✿ 1] with the [Auto Review] item (see page 90). You can select a shorter or longer period, or deactivate Auto review.

Although the feature for instant playback is useful for a quick look, the full Playback mode offers you the ability to take your time and review all of the images stored on your memory card. Access this mode by pressing the Playback button ▶ . Use either the Control dial 🔅 (in front of the shutter button) or the left/right Controller keys to scroll through the images.

To view a photo's histogram on a screen that also includes certain file and shooting information, press the DISP button twice while viewing an image in full playback. Or press the button only once if you simply want to see a full range of data about the settings that were used to make that image. When the camera is in the full Playback mode, pressing the DISP button will also cause the histogram scales to appear. The histograms allow you to evaluate the exposure as discussed in detail on pages 136-141.

There are two additional options in Playback mode that are quite useful. The first is a magnification feature. Use it to check sharpness in specific areas of an image, look for red-eye, gauge facial expressions in people pictures, and so on. In order to magnify an image in Playback mode, press the AEL button located on back of the camera in the top right corner; it's also marked with a magnifying glass and a plus symbol ⊕ . Press it several times for higher magnification. You can now scroll around the image using any of the four keys on the Controller to examine different portions of the enlarged picture.

To decrease magnification, press the exposure compensation button ⊡ (next to the AEL button). It's also marked with a magnifying glass and a minus symbol ⊖ . To return to full image viewing, press the center (AF) button in the middle of the Controller.

Note: In the full Playback ▶ mode, the camera also displays thumbnails of five images in a very small size. If you want to view a specific photo, simply scroll to that using the Controller keys.

The second handy feature is the ability to create an index display for reviewing thumbnails of multiple images. Simply press the exposure compensation ⊡ button while in full image viewing in Playback mode; a new screen will appear showing nine thumbnail photos. This feature is useful to search for a shot stored on your memory card because you can look at more than one picture at a time (although the images are small). You can scroll to a desired photo. If your memory card contains numerous images, continue scrolling past the last displayed photo and the screen will show the next nine photos.

You can also use Playback ▶ mode to review images as a slide show on the LCD monitor with the [Slide Show] item in [Playback Menu 2 ▶ 2], (see page 94 for setup information). Each picture stored on your memory card will display for five seconds before the next image automatically appears. You can shorten or extend the display time for each slide show image with the [Interval] item in the same menu.

Deleting Images

You can delete pictures one at a time in either instant play-back or in the full Playback mode. Simply press the delete button 🗑 (located on back of camera in lower left) while an image is displayed. Scroll using the Controller keys to highlight [YES] on the confirmation screen, then press the center button to complete the single image deletion.

In addition to this feature, the ∝200 provides the ability to delete images that you "mark" for deletion or all images in a folder. Use the Delete feature accessible through [Play-back Menu 1 ▶ 1] to do so (see page 90).

Protect Images from Deletion

Before deleting any images, you may want to protect impor-tant ones from unintentional erasure using the lock feature. You can use the [Protect] item in [Playback Menu 1 ▶ 1] to mark images, and thus protect them from deletion. You can always remove the protection from any image at a later time. See page 91 for details.

The [Format] item in [Playback Menu 1 ▶ 1] will also delete all images on a memory card, through an electronic process that reformats the card. All images, including those protected earlier, will be erased by that process.

Note: Although there is no in-camera method for recovering deleted images, several companies (such as datarescue.com) market software that's designed for this purpose. These programs do not provide a 100% success rate, but some are quite good at recovering deleted JPEGs and, sometimes, RAW files. Some can also recover images—or at least certain images—that were deleted through formatting of the memory card. Look for reviews of such software on the Internet through a web search using keywords such as, "image recovery software programs."

The CCD Imaging Sensor

While the Sony 10MP sensor records images in full color, its individual pixels are actually not able to record color values at all. Each pixel captures a portion of the total light falling on the sensor, and they are only able to record the intensity of the light. Therefore, filters are placed in front of the pixels so each can only record one of the three primary colors (red, green, and blue) of light. These filters are arranged in a specific order, most commonly using the Bayer pattern where there are twice as many green pixels as there are red and blue.

When the light projected by the lens comes into contact with the imaging sensor during exposure, the light-sensitive pixels accumulate an electrical charge. More light striking a particular pixel translates into a stronger electrical charge. The electrical charge for each pixel is converted into a specific value based on the strength of the charge so that the camera can actually process the data. Compared to the earlier $\propto 100$, the $\propto 200$ employs an improved CCD that allows more light to pass through to each pixel increasing sensitivity, reducing digital noise, and providing greater detail.

Because each pixel only records the value of one of the primary colors, full color must be interpolated based on information from adjacent pixels. The final image data is then written to the camera's memory card as an image file. An exception to this would be the RAW capture format, which records raw data (actual pixel values) from the sensor and stores it in a special file format (ARW) that needs to be processed using special software.

In addition to the Bayer pattern filter, a low pass anti-aliasing filter is located in front of the sensor. This reduces the wavy colors and rippled surface patterns (moiré) that can occur when we photograph small, patterned areas with a camera that uses a high-resolution sensor.

The Sensor and Effective Focal Lengths

As with the vast majority of digital cameras, the ∝200's sensor is smaller than a 35mm film frame, which measures 24 x 36 mm. Because of the smaller 23.6 x 15.8 mm size, the view through a lens is different than it would be if mounted on a 35mm camera. Many seasoned photographers like to think in 35mm SLR terms, so they often describe lenses on digital SLRs by their "effective focal lengths." To calculate this effective focal length, multiply by 1.5. For example, a 28–75mm zoom becomes equivalent to a 42–112.5mm zoom in the 35mm format. The smaller sensor reduces the wide-angle capability of the lens, but increases its capacity for telephoto zoom.

This 1.5x factor for effective focal length, or "focal length magnification," is actually a field-of-view crop. In other words, the focal length is not actually increased. The apparent magnification occurs because the small sensor records a smaller portion of the scene than a larger 35mm film frame would. Consequently, the image appears as if it had been taken with a longer lens, one with a narrower field of view that encompasses less of any scene.

This factor is certainly useful in wildlife and sports photography as it reduces the need to use super telephoto lenses

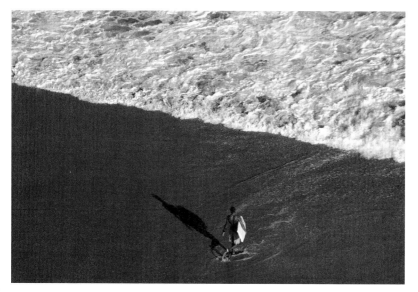

Thanks to the so-called "focal length magnification" factor, even a compact 75-300mm zoom can provide the equivalent of a 450mm focal length. This is very useful when you simply cannot move closer to the subject.

(i.e., 500mm or greater) for tight shots of a distant subject—a moderate telephoto lens (such as the long end of a 75–300mm zoom) will often do the job. But in wide-angle photography, the effective focal length magnification is a drawback because we need extremely short focal lengths to create images with a true ultra-wide effect. That's why Sony is offering shorter, or wider, lenses, such as the 11–18mm zoom; at its short end, this lens provides the ultra-wide field of view that we would expect from a 16.5mm lens on a 35mm camera.

Cleaning the CCD Sensor

Whenever you shut the camera off, the Anti-Dust system will vibrate the CCD sensor to shake loose particles off the filter covering this chip. However, sticky particles or dust in dry climates may remain on the sensor. Prevention of dust accumulation is definitely preferable to cleaning. You'll know if the sensor becomes dusty because spots will appear in your images. In that case, you may decide to clean the sensor. The exact method for doing so requires the use of the Cleaning mode item in the camera's [Setup Menu 3 ↘ 3]; (this process is detailed on pages 98-99).

How to Remove the Memory Card

To remove the memory card, first turn the camera off. Open the card-slot door and find the small card-eject lever; press it once to eject the card; you can then pull it out easily. The lever will stay in the down position so you can close the card-slot door.

Caution: Be certain the red access lamp on back of the camera in the upper right corner is not illuminated. When it is lit, the camera is writing data to the card. Removing a card while data is being recorded can damage the card and cause a permanent loss of image data. To avoid such damage, always turn the camera off before inserting or removing the memory card.

Camera Care and Cleaning

Keep your ∝200 and all lenses clean and well protected when not shooting. Do not expose the camera or lens to water, dust, sand, or salt. A camera bag and a clean, dry storage environment should prevent dust and dirt buildup. Always keep the body cap on the ∝200 when a lens is not mounted; this will prevent dust and contaminants from getting inside the body and settling on the sensor. Keep the front and rear caps on your lenses as well. When you set the camera down, be sure that the lens is not pointing toward the sun, to prevent damage to the CCD sensor.

Always switch the camera off before mounting or removing a lens. This will minimize static electricity, reducing the amount of dust that will be attracted to the

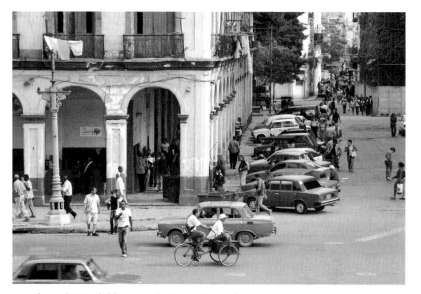

In a photo of this type, dust specks on the sensor would probably not be visible. But in images with a large expanse of light toned areas—such as sky, snow or sand—any imperfections will be obvious.

CCD sensor. When shooting in a location with a great deal of sand or dust, do your best to change lenses quickly in a protected spot. Hold the camera pointing downward when changing lenses. In spite of the automatic sensor cleaning feature, it's still wise to minimize the amount of dust that enters the camera.

In addition, do not leave the camera in hot locations, such as the interior of an automobile parked in the sun. Try to minimize exposure to extreme humidity. In such conditions, keep the camera/lens in a camera bag when not in use.

When storing your ∝200 for more than a week, remove the battery and the memory card. In order to minimize the risk of lost data, do not place the card near a magnet (as in audio speakers) or near any appliance that produces high static electricity discharge. And keep your camera bag immaculately clean; use a vacuum cleaner to remove dust and other contaminants from the bag on a regular basis.

Put together a basic camera care kit, including two microfiber cloths and photographic lens cleaning solution, plus a large blower bulb for blowing dust out of the camera interior. All such accessories are available from photo retail stores. Also carry a soft, absorbent cotton cloth (an old T-shirt perhaps) to dry off the exterior of the camera and lens when working in damp conditions. (Do not shoot in rain or snow unless the camera and lens are well protected.)

Dedicate a microfiber cloth for the purpose of cleaning your lenses; do not use it for other purposes, such as cleaning a smudged LCD monitor; use a cloth of a different color for that. In most cases, a gentle breath of warm air on the front element plus a quick wipe with the microfiber cloth is all you do to clean your lens. To remove stubborn smears or fingerprints, use a photographic lens cleaner solution. Do not use solutions designed for other purposes such as cleaning eyeglass lenses. Apply a drop of solution to a small part of the microfiber cloth; do not pour it onto the front or rear element of the lens because liquid may seep into the optics. Wipe away any of the solution using a clean, dry part of the microfiber cloth.

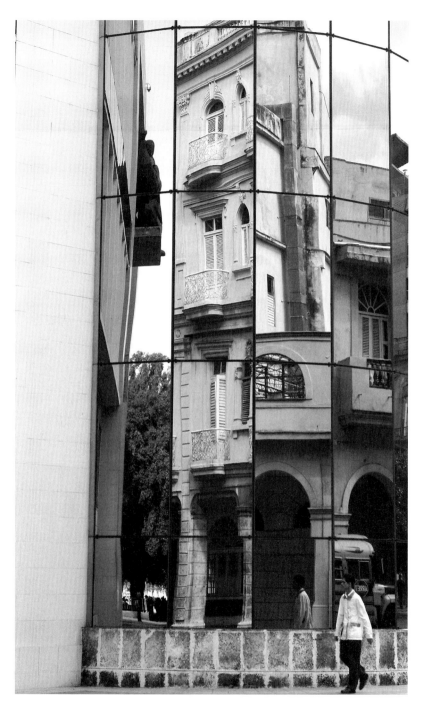

Digital Recording and In-Camera Processing

File Formats

A digital camera processes analog image information from its sensor and converts it to digital data. Typically, the conversion results in 8- or 12-bit color data for each of three different color channels: red, green, and blue. A bit is the smallest piece of information that a computer uses—an acronym for binary digit (0 or 1, off or on).

One great feature of the ∝200 is its ability to record a RAW file in Sony's proprietary ARW format. What sets RAW files apart is that they have undergone little or no internal processing by the camera. These files also contain 12-bit color information, which is considerably more data than an 8-bit JPEG. Also, RAW files offer greater latitude for making corrections during image processing. However, you must use editing software that is compatible with this particular RAW format. Sony bundles just such a program with the camera: Image Data Converter SR. You can also use Adobe Photoshop CS3, Elements version 5.0 or later, or another brand of software that is compatible with Sony's ARW format.

The other recording option with the ∝200 is JPEG. This is an international standard for the compression of images; it reduces the size of a file, allowing more pictures to fit on a memory card. It is also the most common file type created by digital cameras. When a photo is recorded in JPEG form, proprietary processing takes effect. The camera's processor evalu-

↻ *Sony offers a range of options with the ∝200, allowing you to select the capture format: RAW, JPEG, or RAW +JPEG. When shooting JPEGs you can also specify the Quality and the Resolution in order to make the best possible images or to produce smaller files that will consume less space on a memory card.*

ates the 12-bit image, makes adjustments to it, compresses the image, and also reduces color depth to 8-bit. Because this process discards what it deems "redundant" data, JPEG compression is referred to as "lossy." When the file is opened in image editing software, the program will rebuild the JPEG file based on existing data. However, the finer the JPEG quality option that you select, the less original data is discarded.

After the JPEG file is downloaded and enhanced in image editing software, it should be saved as a TIFF or in the image-processing software's native format (such as PhotoShop's PSD). That will prevent further loss of quality that can occur when re-saving a file as JPEG, with additional compression.

Both RAW and JPEG files can give excellent results. The unprocessed data of a RAW file (which can be converted to 16-bit color depth using a RAW converter software program) can be helpful when faced with tough exposure situations, but the small size of the JPEG file is faster and easier to deal with.

The most important factor in deciding which type will work best for you is your own personal shooting and working style. If you want to shoot quickly and spend less time in front of the computer, JPEG might be the best choice. If you loved working in the darkroom and processing film, then RAW is a great continuation of that process. If you are dealing with problematic lighting, shoot in RAW for the superior correction possibilities available with the ARW format files. If you have tons of images to deal with, JPEG may be the most efficient because you will not need to first convert every photo using the special software.

Image Size (Resolution)

For digital cameras, resolution indicates the number of individual pixels contained on the imaging sensor. This is usually expressed in "megapixels" (MP), an abbreviation for millions of pixels. Thus, a 10-megapixel camera has 10 million pixels covering the sensor.

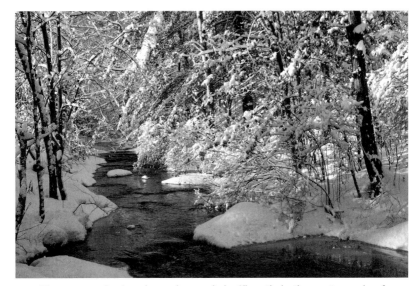

Memory card prices have dropped significantly in the past couple of years, so there's less need to shoot at a lower Size or Quality level. As a rule, you'll want to use RAW or Large/Fine JPEG capture for maximum image quality.

You don't always have to utilize the camera's maximum 10-megapixel resolution. The ∝200 offers the choice of three different JPEG resolution settings, or image sizes, in which to record. Generally it is best to use the highest setting available to take the most finely detailed pictures. This also gives you more flexibility to crop or to make large prints. You can always reduce resolution later with image-processing software in the computer.

Below are the three options available when selecting JPEG image size. (RAW capture will always utilize the full 10 megapixels.) Scroll to the [Image Size] item in [Recording Menu 1 ◘ 1] with the Controller keys, press the central AF button, scroll to the desired image size option and press the AF button again to confirm your selection. Choose from one of the following for JPEG capture:

- **Large (L:10M):** 3872 pixels x 2592 pixels (approximately 10.2 megapixels)
- **Medium (M:5.6M):** 2896 x 1936 pixels (5.6 megapixels)
- **Small (S:2.5M):** 1920 x 1280 pixels (2.5 megapixels)

There may be situations where it is preferable to shoot at less than maximum resolution. Lower resolution (smaller) image files save storage space and processing time. You can fit more of them on your memory card than those captured using higher resolution settings. Smaller files used in emails or on web pages can be handled by servers and browsers more easily and quickly than large files. Do note, however, that even a Small 2.5 megapixel file is probably larger than you would want to use on a Web site; it would need to be downsized further in image editing software.

Image Quality (Compression)

Image quality refers to the amount of compression you want the in-camera processing engine to apply. Compression reduces the size of the files recorded to the memory card; the greater the compression, the lower the quality of the file. Four options are available under the [Quality] item in [Recording Menu 1 📷 1]. This is the full list:

- **RAW:** (ARW format) Some "lossless" compression is auto-matically applied; the image maintains full quality.
- **RAW+J (JPEG):** Full quality for the RAW capture and the least amount of JPEG compression (JPEG Fine).
- **Fine:** Applies the least amount of compression to JPEG files in order to maintain high quality.
- **Standard:** Applies a higher amount of compression to JPEGs, resulting in lower quality files.

ARW Format RAW Files

When you record using the camera's RAW mode, the files are always created at the maximum resolution of 10.2 MP. They also receive little in-camera processing and contain more color and tone information than JPEGs. Consequently, they are significantly larger and consume more memory in both your card and your computer. I recommend a high

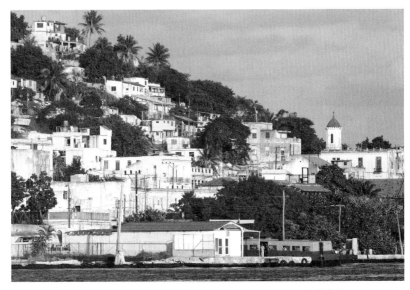

The RAW capture mode is particularly useful in difficult lighting con-ditions such as this, with dark shadows and very bright highlight areas. Use RAW capture and you can modify a photo quite exten-sively—with a non-destructive process—before converting it to TIFF or JPEG.

capacity memory card, at least 2 gigabytes (GB), if you plan to frequently shoot in RAW format.

Because the ARW format is not compatible with all image-processing programs, special software must be used to convert these files to a format (such as TIFF) that is recognized by standard image-processing programs. The Sony Image Data Converter SR software will work, but you can also use other image-processing programs, such as Adobe Photoshop CS3, Lightroom or Elements version 5.0 or higher.

These ARW files offer greater dynamic range (latitude) than JPEGs, as well as more flexibility in computer process-ing to affect exposure, color temperature, white balance, color saturation, and contrast. You have more options about how to process and use that information than you do with JPEGs. However, in RAW capture, you can shoot only six or seven photos in a single series at 3 frames per second (fps). After that, the framing rate slows to about 2 fps; of course, you can shoot many additional photos at this rate when using a high speed memory card.

RAW+JPEG Recording

As indicated earlier, the ∝200 gives you the option to shoot a RAW file plus a JPEG image at the same time in the [Quality] item. That will generate a largest/finest JPEG along with the naturally large RAW file. The JPEG size and quality are "fixed" to Large/Fine in the RAW+JPEG mode and cannot be changed (as is possible in some other brands of cameras).

The RAW+JPEG recording mode can be useful if you want JPEGs for making prints quickly as well as RAW files for later processing in your RAW converter software. The combination of RAW and JPEG means a great deal of data that must be recorded to the memory card. Hence, this option will fill your card quickly and you will be able to shoot fewer images in a sequence at the full 3 fps rate because of all the extra processing that the camera must complete. When using a high speed memory card, you can shoot additional photos (after the first three) but the framing rate will be noticeably slower.

JPEG Files

The ∝200 provides two distinct JPEG options under the [Quality] item, available in [Recording Menu 1 📷 1]. Select [Fine] and the processor will use less compression than it would with the [Standard] option, so the file will be larger. The Standard option might be useful at times—when you don't have much capacity left on your memory card, for example. However, be aware that increased compression creates an image that is less fine. When data is restored and highly compressed Standard files are opened, some "artifacts," such as jagged subject edges, may appear.

Regardless of the JPEG Size/Quality combination that you select, the camera will be able to shoot a very long series of images at 3fps. With a high-speed memory card, it should keep taking photos until the card is full.

Note: Both JPEG and RAW files include data about all camera settings in compliance with EXIF 2.2 (EXIF stands for Exchangeable Image File Format). This allows you to check shooting data when viewing an image in-camera and also in a computer. The EXIF data is also employed by some printers when printing directly from the camera via a USB cable.

Approximate File Sizes

The chart below shows the size of files in megabytes (MB) with the various formats, quality, and resolution options offered by the ∝200. These are approximate since file size can vary depending on the amount of fine detail in an image.

Quality	Large	Medium	Small
ARW (RAW)	9.58 MB	NA	NA
JPEG Fine	3.71 MB	2.97 MB	0.98 MB
JPEG Standard	2.4 MB	1.32 MB	0.67 MB
RAW & JPEG	13.29 MB (9.58 + 3.71)	NA	NA

Do note that these are the file sizes stored on the memory card. When you later open a JPEG in your computer, the JPEG compression will be reversed: Your imaging program will reconstitute the data (by adding pixels) that was discarded during in-camera processing. Hence, the in-computer JPEG file will be much larger. For example, a Large/Fine JPEG will be a full 28.7 MB in size. A RAW file will also be much larger after it is processed by the special converter software and converted to a format such as TIFF; the file will then be about 28.7 MB in size.

16:9 Aspect Ratio

By default, the ∝200 generates photos in a typical 3:2 format that produces the largest possible images in terms of the number of pixels, as discussed in the previous section. However, Sony also provides a 16:9 aspect ratio for making longer/narrower images that conform to the shape of a widescreen TV monitor. This alternative can be selected with the [Aspect Ratio] item in [Recording Menu I 📷 1]. That can be useful if you plan to display your photos for friends on a large television monitor.

Do note, however, that the long/narrow format is not ideal for making prints on standard paper sizes. As well, the image size's pixel count will be smaller because the camera crops (eliminates) part of the actual photo. Hence, it's better to always use the standard 3:2 option and crop any photos that you want to display on a wide screen TV using image editing software.

The actual image sizes in the 16:9 format will be as follows:

RAW capture or Large JPEG: 3872 x 2176 pixels (8.4MP)
Medium JPEG: 2896 x 1632 (4.7MP)
Small JPEG: 1920 x 1088 (2.1MP)

Memory Card Capacity
The following estimates—for images made in the 3:2 aspect ratio—are approximate since actual file size can vary depending on the amount of fine detail in an image. These values apply to the use of a 1GB memory card.

Quality	Size	Approx photo files per card
ARW (RAW)	NA	65
JPEG Fine	Large	242
JPEG Standard	Large	377
JPEG Fine	Medium	419
JPEG Standard	Medium	640
JPEG Fine	Small	867
JPEG Standard	Small	1262
RAW & JPEG		51 RAW and 51 JPEG

Benefits of RAW Capture

The amount of data in RAW files allows more adjustment latitude in image-processing software for color, white balance, contrast, and exposure without file degradation that can occur with JPEGs due to over processing in the computer. Generally, you can also expect more pleasing prints at larger sizes (e.g. 13 x 19 inches [33 x 48 cm]) from files originally shot in RAW.

Note: In RAW capture, the camera's processor records the in-camera settings used for aspects such as color saturation, color mode, contrast, white balance, and sharpness. However, those aspects are not actually locked into the RAW file by the camera as they are with JPEGs. Hence, you can retain the in-camera settings or change them as desired with a RAW converter software program.

Let's say you are shooting inside a stadium under sodium-vapor lighting and you forget to change from Automatic White Balance. At the end of the day you notice all your images exhibit a strong color cast. Or perhaps your exposure was a bit off for some of the shots at one end of the field. You'll usually have better results correcting these types of problems (using ARW format compatible software) if you were shooting in RAW capture mode.

While no software can work miracles with a grossly over or underexposed image, you should be able to correct moderate exposure errors (plus or minus one stop or EV) without giving the RAW image an artificial look. Major changes can also be made to other aspects of an image, such as color, contrast, and white balance, without negative effects on the pixels.

Yet working with RAW does have certain drawbacks. The larger RAW files consume more space on a memory card than JPEGs. In addition, converting and adjusting ARW format files—before a final fine-tuning in your conventional imaging software—adds extra post-processing time. That can be a problem after you return from a long trip with hundreds of images.

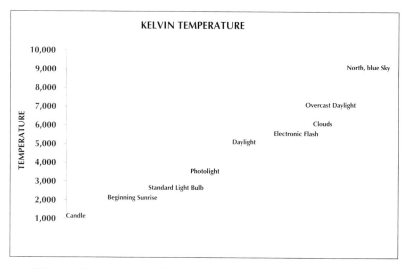

KELVIN TEMPERATURE

TEMPERATURE

10,000	
9,000	North, blue Sky
8,000	
7,000	Overcast Daylight
6,000	Clouds
	Electronic Flash
5,000	Daylight
4,000	
	Photolight
3,000	
	Standard Light Bulb
2,000	Beginning Sunrise
1,000	Candle

Although it's not essential to become intimate with the Kelvin scale, this chart provides an indication as to the color temperature of various types of light. The camera's AWB and WB preset modes do try to compensate to produce images with "accurate" white balance. When these do not meet your needs, switch to the WB overrides discussed in this chapter.

The choice between RAW and JPEG is up to you. Determine the advantages and limitations of each and use what works best for your shooting style or each shooting situation.

White Balance

Unlike the film used in conventional cameras, the sensors in digital cameras can be adjusted for different color temperatures of light. In other words, we can cause the camera to produce a natural-looking image, rendering whites as pure white in various types of lighting. When the whites are accurate, other tones are accurate as well, without a strong color cast. This is known as adjusting the white balance (WB).

White Balance—How It Works

Every light source emits a different range of wavelengths, varying from primarily short (appearing blue) to primarily long (appearing red.) Even the light from the sun can vary. It is cooler (bluer) on overcast days than during a sunrise or sunset (warmer, redder). While our brain perceptually adjusts for these differences, photographic film and digital sensors record them more objectively.

The color of light is defined numerically using the Kelvin color temperature scale. Lower Kelvin temperatures denote the warm, reddish light produced by a bonfire, an incandescent lamp, and the sun when it is low in the sky. Higher Kelvin temperatures denote the cool, bluish light at twilight, on heavily overcast days, or in a shady area.

On the Kelvin scale, full sunlight (mid day) is typically between 5100K and 5500K. The light on an overcast day is usually between 5500K and 6500K. In full shade, the light is even bluer: typically between 7000K and 8000K. The range provided for these different types of light is quite broad because it's affected by the exact time of day, the extent of the clouds that filter the light from the sun, the time of year, and atmospheric factors such as haze, smog, fog, or dust particles in the air.

Artificial light sources also produce light with certain color temperatures. Household tungsten lamps produce light with an orange cast (about 3200K). Most fluorescent tubes produce greenish light. Unusual lamps, such as sodium vapor and mercury vapor, produce light with a strange color that can be difficult to define.

In order to produce images with clean whites (and hence, accurate tones overall), digital cameras can be adjusted for the specific color temperature produced by these various light sources. This is referred to as white balance (WB). You can set WB with your ∝200, including an option called Auto White Balance (AWB) that attempts to automatically detect the type of existing light.

Your ∝200 provides additional options for controlling white balance in a broad variety of lighting conditions. Some of the advanced features are straightforward and intuitive. Others are complex, of the type you would expect in a camera designed for professional photographers. While you may not plan to use all of the options, it's worth understanding how they work and why they might be useful.

To select from the white balance options, press the **Fn** button to access the Function sub-menu. Scroll to the [White balance] item and press the AF button in the center of the Controller. A list of White Balance options now appears. Scroll down to the one you want to use with the Controller keys or the camera's Control dial. When you reach the one that is closest to the actual lighting conditions, press the AF button to enter and confirm your selection.

Auto White Balance AWB

This option is designed to analyze the color of light and set an appropriate color temperature to render whites as white. This system works quite well outdoors, especially on sunny or partly cloudy days, and indoors with flash. It's an especially useful choice when the light is changing rapidly (from sunny to cloudy to sunny again), or when shooting subjects that move from one type of lighting to another—sunlight to shadow, for example. But AWB does not always work so well under manufactured lighting such as tungsten or sodium vapor.

Preset White Balance Selections

You can usually get more accurate white balance rendition in mixed or artificial lighting than AWB by selecting a specific WB setting—called a preset—designed specifically for those conditions.

To select a preset WB, scroll down to the second option in the [White balance] list and then scroll right. Now, several white balance preset options will be visible, each with an icon and a description in words: [Daylight ☀], [Shade 🏠], [Cloudy ☁], [Tungsten (household lamps) 💡], [Fluorescent 💡], and [Flash WB⚡]. (Two other options are available, [Color Temperature] and [Custom WB] discussed shortly on page 68.)

Note: When using flash merely to lighten shadows in a scene where sunlight (or another light source) is the primary source of illumination, do not select the Flash WB WB⚡ preset. Instead, use AWB or make your white balance selection based on the type of illumination that is the main light source for the shot. Reserve the Flash WB WB⚡ preset for low light photography when the subject will be primarily lit by the electronic flash.

WB Levels Adjustment: You can fine-tune the white balance level of any of the White Balance presets. Scroll to the right from any WB preset; then scroll left/right to modify the amount of levels adjustment. Select a plus [+] factor for a warmer (more red/yellow) effect. Or set a minus [-] factor for a cooler (more bluish) effect. You can make adjustments within a range from +3 to -3.

You may find the WB levels adjustment option useful; however, there is no way to determine the effect that any specific setting will produce before you take a photo. Hence, this feature calls for a lot of trial-and-error experimentation. You may decide to permanently leave the ∝200 set to a -1 factor for Cloudy WB ☁ if you find that the camera routinely makes images that are slightly too yellow on overcast days, for example. Or permanently set a +1 factor for Flash WB WB⚡ if you find the camera routinely produces images that are slightly too blue when using flash.

Once you have set a WB level adjustment, the camera will retain that setting until you readjust it, even after turning the camera off. It will be used whenever you select a specific white balance preset in the future.

Hint: WB levels adjustment is not very scientific because the exact color of light often varies within a broad range, as on a cloudy day, for example. When shooting in lighting conditions where the camera routinely makes images with inaccurate white balance, I strongly recommend using the Custom WB ⬛ feature (discussed below) instead.

Creative Use of Preset White Balance: Using the "wrong" white balance setting can yield some interesting creative effects. For example, the ⬛ preset can be used when the sun is shining brightly to create an effect resembling that produced by a pale warming filter. For a stronger warming effect, try the ⬛ preset; that will produce a very obvious yellow/orange color cast.

The tungsten WB ⬛ preset produces the opposite—a strong blue cast, useful with some winter scenes for a much "cooler" effect. Experiment with using the various preset choices for creative purposes. You can always check the results in the camera's LCD monitor.

Custom White Balance ⬛

Scroll down to the final item in the [White balance] list if you want to use this feature to set the white balance value for any type of lighting. (In simplified terms, this feature teaches the camera to render whites as white regardless of the color of the light. When whites are accurate, other colors will appear natural as well.) Though a sophisticated function, it is not overly complicated to set. It is well worth the bit of extra effort to learn because this feature virtually guarantees good white balance under any unusual or tricky lighting condition.

While Sony provides a full range of WB overrides, the AWB system is *often reliable in the circumstances where we typically take most photos: outdoors in sunny or cloudy conditions, with or without flash (used for lightening shadow areas).*

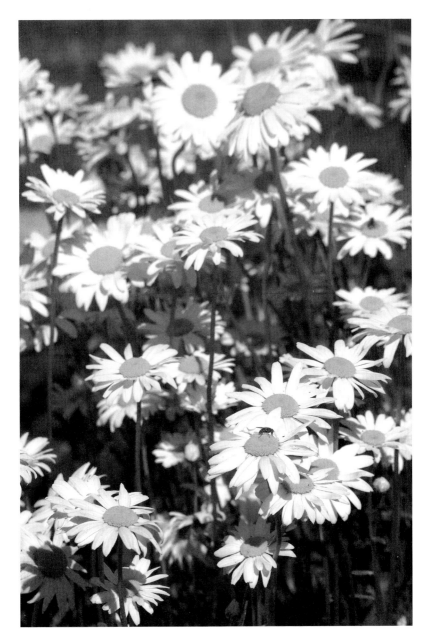

For Custom WB, a sheet of white paper or a gray card is needed as a target in order to calibrate the camera. In order to set Custom White Balance for a specific lighting condition, follow these steps exactly as specified. It is a good idea to photocopy them for handy reference while you're out shooting.

1. Place the white sheet of paper (or gray card) in the same light that will illuminate the most important part of the subject when you take your planned photo. (For a portrait for example, ask the person to hold the sheet or card at his or her face.)

2. In the Function sub-menu, scroll to [White balance] with the Controller and press the central AF button; then scroll down to [Custom]. Scroll to the right to the [SET] option and press the central AF button.

3. Look through the viewfinder and point the lens so the central area of the frame (within the circle etched on the viewing screen) is filled with your white or gray target. Be careful not to cast a shadow over your target. The white or gray sheet does not need to be in focus. If the autofocus system keeps trying to focus without success, switch to manual focus with the AF/MF control on the front of the camera.

4. Press the shutter button all the way down. The camera will take a photo of your white or gray target. When it does so, it also calibrates the WB system; in other words, it registers the settings required for accurate white balance under the specific lighting conditions. An image of your target will now appear in the LCD monitor with the words "Custom white balance" above it.

If the image looks neutral—without a color cast caused by the lights illuminating the subject—the calibration process has been successful. If not, turn the camera off and back on. Restart the calibration process.

When calibration is finished, the camera is set for Custom WB ![icon]. You can now remove the white sheet or grey card from the scene. Switch back to autofocus if you had previously set manual focus. Recompose to take the desired photos. As long as the type and color of the lighting does not change, you can keep taking photos and get accurate white balance.

On rare occasions, you'll get a "Custom WB error" message in the LCD monitor indicating that the system cannot calibrate under the existing conditions. This is most likely to occur when a white target is illuminated by extremely bright light or if you used flash for the calibration process. In that case, try again after pushing the flash back into the down position. If you again get an error message in extremely bright light, you will need to calibrate using a gray card because it reflects less light; the calibration process should then be successful.

When flash is active during the calibration procedure, the camera may not be able to complete the procedure. (That is most likely to occur when the flash was very close to the white sheet or the grey card.) If the process fails, the camera will revert to normal operation after step 4, without registering the Custom WB settings. In that case, turn the flash off or push the built-in flash back into the down position and try again. (While setting Custom WB, use the camera's P, A, S, or M exposure mode so the flash will not automatically pop up and fire in low light.)

Note: It is sometimes possible to complete full calibration even when flash is used during the process. To do so, you must not be too close to the white sheet or the grey card. (Zoom in on the target with a longer focal length setting on a zoom lens.) You may find Custom WB in flash photography to be useful when shooting in a location where the subject will be illuminated by very bright artificial lights as well as the flash. In low light conditions—where flash is obviously the primary light source—that is unnecessary; you can get very nice white balance with AWB or the Flash WB preset.

The ∝200 saves the last custom WB setting even when the camera is turned off or switched to another WB option. At any future time, scrolling to the Custom WB will cause the camera to automatically recall the WB setting you had previously set. This can be useful if you often return to shoot in the same sports arena, for example, where the lighting is always the same.

If you decide to take photos in entirely different lighting with Custom WB, you will need to re-calibrate the system. Scroll to the right to the [SET] option and repeat the calibration procedure for the new lighting conditions as per the six steps shown previously.

Color Temperature
This option allows you to set a specific Kelvin color temperature for white balance purposes. It is intended for photographers who use a color temperature meter or shoot under lighting with a known color temperature, or who follow the manufacturer's recommendations for certain types of lighting. If you aren't using these methods, the camera's other white balance options will be more useful.

To try this feature, scroll down to the [Color Temperature] item; [5500k] (or some other K number) will appear on the right side of the LCD screen. Scroll to the right or to the left to set a higher or lower K number. If you also want to apply filtration, scroll down one step from the [K number] to the [Color Filter] item. This is a magenta/green compensation feature that can be used to adjust the white balance toward either magenta or green as if you were using filters over the lens, as in traditional film photography. (This feature is most helpful for fine tuning white balance for fluorescent bulbs, which tend to produce a green color cast.)

Scroll left to set a [G] option if you want to add a green tint to your image; select the desired intensity from G1 (mild) to G5 (strong). Or scroll right to set an [M] option, for a magenta tint to the desired intensity from M1 to M5.

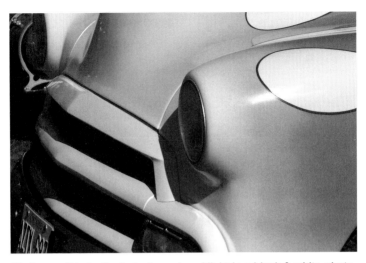

It's impossible to illustrate the color of light in a black & white photo, but this image was made around sunset when the light was quite amber in color. While AWB provided a rich, warm effect, the Color Temperature option was useful for quickly producing more accurate white balance for documenting the true colors of this classic car.

White Balance Bracketing

When white balance bracketing is active, the camera generates three image files of a scene, each at a slightly different white balance setting. It's available with all of the WB options when shooting JPEGs. (It is not necessary with RAW since you can easily change the color temperature when processing your ARW files.)

Access this feature by pressing the drive button on the top of the camera ▯ . A screen with various options will appear on the LCD monitor. Using the Controller keys or the Control dial, scroll to the ▯Lo item. The words WB Bracket will be displayed on the right side of the LCD screen.

The WB Lo option will produce a slight variance in color temperature for each of the three photos. A second option is also available, ▯Hi, for a greater variance in color temperature. You can select that by scrolling to the right with the Controller key. After making your selection, press the central AF button to enter and confirm your choice.

When you take a single shot, the camera's processing system automatically generates the original image file plus two copies, each with a slightly different white balance adjustment. (Only the last of the three images will be displayed on the LCD monitor, but you can view all three in the camera's Playback mode.) One duplicate image will be slightly warmer (red/yellow) while the other will be slightly cooler (blue). The difference will be most obvious if you were using the [Hi] white balance bracketing option.

In my experience, this feature is most appropriate when using one of the preset white balance options. (Set the desired preset first, before setting the WB bracketing.) It increases the odds of getting an image with the most pleasing color. This feature has some disadvantages: it's available only with Single frame ☐ advance; the extra two files consume more space on a memory card; and though it takes less than a second, the extra processing time may cause you to miss a fleeting gesture in candid picture taking.

Creative Styles

The ∝200 provides a wide range of Creative Styles; each provides a different effect. Select the one that is most appropriate for a certain type of scene. Check out the available options in [Recording Menu 1 ■ 1] by scrolling down to the [Creative Style] item and pressing the AF button. When the new screen appears, scroll down to see all of the options: [Standard Standard]], [Vivid Vivid], [Portrait Portrait], [Landscape Landscape], [Night View Night], [Sunset Sunset], [B/W B/W], and [Adobe Adobe]. Select the one you want and press the AF button to confirm your decision. Each will be discussed in a moment.

Note: The Creative Style menu item cannot be selected when the camera is set to one of the fully automatic, subject-specific Scene modes. For experimenting with the various options, set the camera to the M, S, A, or P exposure mode. In the fully automatic Scene modes, the camera makes the "appropriate" settings. For example, it may pro-

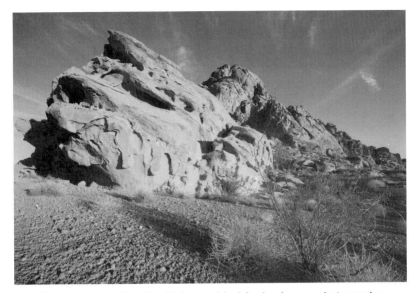

The Landscape Creative Style was ideal for landscape photography, producing a very striking effect. Naturally, no one option is ideal for all types of subjects. For instance, the Landscape Creative Style renders skin tones with exaggerated saturation that is unlikely to be appreciated by a portrait subject. That's why Sony provides a full range of options and user-selectable overrides for Contrast, Color Saturation, and Sharpness.

vide a warmer color balance, higher color saturation, and more contrast when taking a photo in Landscape Scene mode than it would in Portrait Scene mode. In the Scene modes, the camera's processor makes all such decisions and provides no indication of the effects that it will produce.

Let's take a closer look at the effects that the camera will provide when you select any of the Creative Style modes. They are primarily intended for JPEG capture because when you shoot in RAW capture, you can modify any aspect of an image later, using special converter software.

Standard Standard⁺ : This is an all-purpose mode that produces JPEGs with rich, faithful colors, and moderately high sharpness and contrast.

Vivid Vivid⁺ : This option generates images with "deep and vivid" colors most appropriate with landscapes where a particularly bold color rendition is desirable. It is less suitable for portraits because skin tones will not appear natural.

Portrait Portrait⁺ : This mode is optimized for the reproduction of skin tones. In-camera contrast, sharpness, and color saturation are slightly reduced for a softer, more flattering effect with natural (not overly rich) colors.

Landscape Landscape⁺ : This mode reproduces outdoor scenes with higher than average contrast, color saturation, and sharpness. Similar to Vivid, it produces "punchier" images. Especially in reds, color saturation is so high that there can be loss of fine detail (for example in flower petals).

Night View Night⁺ : Intended for taking night scene photos without flash, this mode is said to modify contrast and color for a pleasing effect. In low light I found this mode similar to Standard, although Night View provides slightly higher contrast and deeper color tones.

Sunset Sunset⁺ : Optimized for landscapes at dusk and dawn, this produces a red/yellow color cast when used in daytime shooting. Contrast and color saturation are automatically increased slightly to produce a sunrise or sunset photo with a warm rich glow as well as high color richness.

Black & White B/W⁺ : When selected, the images will be monochrome and not in color. The tones are neutral and the overall effect is suitable for making prints without adjustments in image-processing software. However, serious black-and-white photographers will want to adjust Levels and other controls in their imaging software to produce the exact desired effect.

Adobe RGB Adobe⁺ : This is the only camera option that will produce images in the Adobe RGB color space (see Color Space, below), with a wider color gamut (recording range) than sRGB. This is useful for making inkjet prints. However, when viewed on a computer monitor, Adobe RGB exhibits less rich colors than sRGB.

Color Space

Digital cameras render color based on combinations of red, blue, and green and in terms of hue, saturation, and brightness. The various systems that define these colors are called color spaces. Color spaces were invented with different biases based largely on how images will be created or viewed. Two color spaces are common in digital imaging: sRGB and Adobe RGB. By default, the ∝200 always employs the sRGB color space; that is ideal for on-screen viewing and Internet use. It's also the color space that's preferred for print making by most of the mass market photofinishing labs.

Adobe RGB is an entirely different color space, able to record a wider range of colors. It's used by the camera only when you select Adobe as the desired Creative Style.

Adobe RGB vs. sRGB Color Space

The camera always employs the sRGB color space unless you specifically select the ⌷Adobe⌷ Creative Style. The Adobe RGB mode provides a wider "gamut" or range of recorded colors; that is ideal for inkjet print making. However, many image editing software programs do not provide support for the Adobe RGB color space; the Sony and Adobe programs do so, as well as some others. Programs that are incompatible with Adobe RGB will convert the images to the standard sRGB color space, produce an "incompatible color space" error message, or generate an inaccurate display of the colors. If you are not certain that your favorite imaging software supports the Adobe RGB color space, then do not select this Creative Style.

Note too that most commercial printing firms are optimized for printing sRGB images because this is the most popular color space. Hence, you won't want to use Adobe RGB for images that you take or send to a high-volume printing lab (photofinishers, on-line printing services, etc.). Some labs will be able to handle such images but may convert them to the sRGB color space before making the actual prints. On the other hand, labs offering professional-quality custom printing often use the Adobe RGB color space, taking advantage of its wider color gamut. If you use any print-making services, ask them which color space they prefer.

Optimizing Images In-Camera
While scrolling through the Creative Styles, you probably noticed other options on the right side of the LCD screen, along the bottom of the display. These consist of three icons for Contrast ◐ , Color saturation ◉ , and Sharpness ⬚ , respectively. Scrolling to the right from any Creative Style option allows you to modify the level of each of these image "parameters" or attributes from very high to very low. (There's no need for this feature if shooting in RAW format because the images can be adjusted in the converter software before conversion to another format.)

In-camera image optimization is particularly useful if you shoot JPEGs and print directly from the camera or a memory card. If you fall into this category, or if you do not want to spend time optimizing contrast, color saturation, and sharpness in a computer, you may wish to do so in-camera. Simply scroll to the right from any [Creative Style] mode option and then scroll to the [Contrast ◐], [Color saturation ◉], and [Sharpness ⬚] options. Then, you can scroll up to boost the level of this parameter to a [+] setting for a stronger effect or scroll down for a more moderate level to a [–] setting for a milder effect.

Let's take a look at each of the three and why you may wish to adjust its level of intensity. Do note that for all three, the default level is zero: a mild intensity. The user selectable levels range from -3 to +3.

Contrast ◐ : To reduce contrast in harsh lighting conditions or to create flattering portraits that benefit from a soft look, you may want to set Contrast to -1 or to -2. That is also useful for any type of photo to minimize the loss of detail in highlight and shadow areas in harsh lighting.

In flat light, such as an overcast day, you might want to try a +1 level for more separation of light to dark elements. Think twice about selecting a higher contrast level for any other type of lighting. Low contrast is easy to fix in image-processing software, but excessive contrast can be difficult to moderate without creating an artificial-looking effect. In fact, you may want to permanently set a –1 level if you plan to enhance your photos in image-processing software.

Color Saturation ⊕ : The ∝200 often produces images with just the right color richness or vibrancy for many types of subjects when you use the appropriate Creative Style mode. Of course, you may decide that you prefer a less intense color effect for a landscape for a more muted overall look or to avoid the loss of detail in excessively rich colors. (When using a polarizing filter over the lens, color satura-tion can be especially vivid—not always the desired effect.) That's easy to achieve by setting Color Saturation to a -1, or even a -2 level.

On the other hand, you might want more vivid colors for portraits of a group of circus clowns, for example. In that case, when using the Portrait Creative Style, you might set a +1 level for Color Saturation.

Note: I find that a –1 saturation level (in Standard or Adobe RGB Creative Style) produces color that is preferable for the majority of subjects, but this is a subjective judgment. If you plan to extensively manipulate your JPEG photos in image-processing software, you'll probably want to start with a –1 or –2 Color Saturation level in-camera. Think twice about selecting a high saturation level; excessive color saturation can lead to loss of detail; that problem can be very difficult to correct later in the computer.

Sharpness ⊞ : The camera produces slightly soft images in many of the Creative Styles but it boosts sharpness automatically in some Styles, especially Landscape. If you find that you prefer stronger sharpening—for all photos or in a specific situation—simply increase that parameter to +1 or perhaps to +2 for a more obvious effect. This is particularly useful for those who often make prints without first modifying the images in a computer program.

Again, it's easier to increase sharpness in image editing software than to moderate this aspect. Many programs provide several advanced sharpening tools that produce an even more natural sharpening effect. They usually provide full control, in small increments as to the extent of sharpening, to produce the perfect effect for any particular subject and for a specific print size that you will make or order. If you plan to take advantage of these tools, do not set a higher in-camera sharpening level; in fact, some Photoshop experts prefer to set a -3 level in-camera and provide all sharpening during "post-processing" in a computer.

In my experience, a -1 setting for Sharpness works well enough to produce sharp, but not artificially sharp, images. Before making a print, I'll apply Unsharp Mask or Smart Sharpen in Photoshop or Elements, selecting exactly the amount that is appropriate for the subject and the print size.

D-Range Optimizer (DRO)

This feature is provided by the camera's BIONZ processor and creates images with an optimized level for exposure and contrast. At default, the [Standard D-R] mode is used but you can also select [Advanced D-R+] or [Off D-OFF]. (When Off is selected, the processor does not take extra steps to correct brightness or contrast.) To find this feature, press the Fn button, scroll to [D-Range Optimizer] item, press the central AF button and then scroll to the desired option. Press the AF button again to confirm your selection.

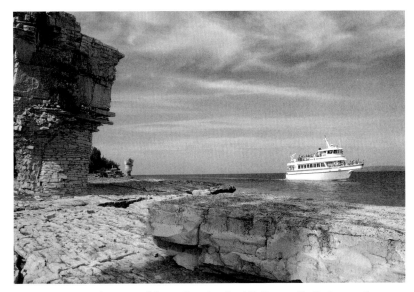

In most outdoor conditions, the standard D-Range Optimizer option produces very good JPEGs, but in high contrast lighting, you may also want to take a photo using the Advanced option. Each image will differ in exposure and contrast; simply use the one that you consider to be the best.

According to Sony, "DRO modifies the range from high-lights to shadows, including gain and contrast, through its in-camera hardware processing to produce more natural, evenly exposed pictures. The camera's image analysis technology studies the captured image data and instantly determines the best exposure and color tonality for the image before JPEG compression." More specifically, here's what you can expect when using one of the two D-Range Optimizer modes.

Standard **D-R** : The basic DRO mode, its primary purpose is to recover shadow detail in scenes with a lot of contrast. For example, the scene may include a very bright sky and a darker landscape. Standard DRO will lighten the shadow areas for a more pleasing overall exposure. The extra processing takes very little time and operation will not slow down.

Advanced ▣ : In this more sophisticated mode, the camera analyzes 1200 individual segments of the scene and adjusts brightness only in specific areas of the image. Then the processor will lighten shadow areas and darken very bright areas in order to bring out detail in both for a more pleasing overall effect. This extra processing does take some time, so the camera's framing rate will not be the full 3 fps. In other respects, you won't likely notice any slowdown; the ∝200 will still usually be ready to take a few shots, even while it is recording previous images to the memory card.

When the camera is set to any of the subject-specific Scene modes, the processor automatically sets either the Standard ▣ or the Advanced DRO ▣ mode, but you can select either of the other options as well. Do note, however, that the camera will revert to its preferred choice as soon as the camera turns off, goes into power-saving Sleep mode, or when you switch to another exposure mode. Frankly, when using the camera in a fully automatic mode, it makes sense to allow it to make all of its own settings. Switch to the P, A, or S mode if you want full control.

Note: D-Range Optimizer will not produce any effect when the camera is set to RAW, RAW+JPEG capture, when the exposure mode is set to Manual, or when either Spot or Center weighted metering is in use. That's fine, because this function is really a problem-solving tool that is unnecessary for many photos. Also, exposure, contrast, and highlight/shadow detail can be modified as desired in the computer, using the special converter software program.

The result of DRO can vary from subtle to obvious. Try experimenting with both of its modes to determine whether you appreciate the effect that each produces or whether you prefer to make the necessary exposure/contrast changes yourself, using other in-camera features or image-processing software. Once you have a better understanding of the effect that each mode provides, you'll know when to select one of the DRO options and when to turn it Off ▣ .

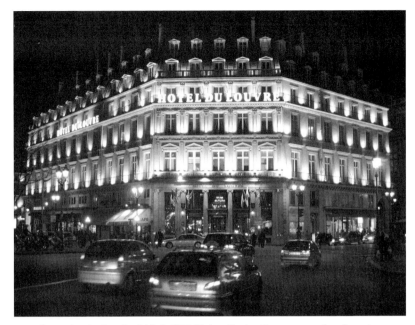

A moderate level of High ISO Noise Reduction processing is automatically applied by the camera's BIONZ engine at ISO 1600 and ISO 3200 (in single frame Drive mode), minimizing the "graininess" in such images. This is a useful feature, but it can be turned off; the resulting images will exhibit more obvious noise but slightly higher resolution of fine detail.

Noise Reduction

Digital images made using long exposures (over one second) can exhibit noticeable digital noise even when low ISO settings are used. A similar effect can become obvious when we shoot at very high ISO levels, especially at ISO 1600 and higher. Digital noise is similar to the grain we see in prints made with high-speed films, but the specks are more colorful. The "noise pattern" is most visible in mid-tone areas or in dark areas that are lightened with image-processing software.

The camera's CCD sensor and BIONZ processor combine to produce "clean" images in most circumstances and applies

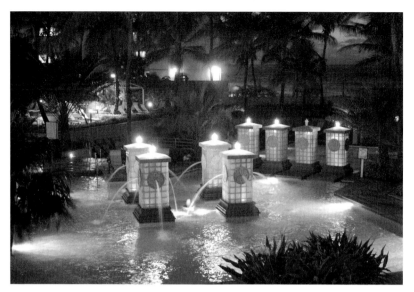

Long Exposure NR is activated only when the shutter speed is 1 second or longer. This feature is useful for making "cleaner" images, but it does produce a delay while the additional processing is applied. If you often make very long exposures, experiment with the effect you'll get with and without NR to determine which you prefer.

extra noise reduction (NR) processing to images made at a shutter speed of 1 second or longer and in images made at ISO levels from 1600 to 3200. That additional processing minimizes the "grainy" effect; both the sharpness and the color of the specks are moderated. Both NR features are active by default but only in single frame ▭ advance. The extra NR processing is deactivated if the camera is set in continuous advance or continuous bracketing drive.

Either or both of the noise reduction features can also be turned off. To do so, scroll down to the [Long Exposure NR] and then to the [High ISO NR] item in [Recording Menu 2 ▸ 2]. Press the AF button and scroll down to [Off]; press the AF button again to confirm your selection.

If you often make long exposures, as in night photography, or often shoot at ISO 1600 to 3200, you may appreciate the Noise Reduction features. However, they do produce some drawbacks:

1. The entire image becomes slightly softer than it would be without the extra noise reduction processing. Actual resolution can also suffer. That can be corrected to a degree with the in-camera control for increasing sharpness or, preferably, in a computer using image-processing software.

2. There is a delay after you take a shot while the Long Exposure NR feature is on: 1 second for a 1 second exposure, 10 seconds for a 10 second exposure, and so on. During this time the camera is not operable, which can be quite frustrating. The extra processing is not nearly as long with High ISO NR; it takes about a quarter of a second.

Before any serious photography with very long shutter speeds or at very high ISO levels, I strongly recommend some experimentation. Find a low light scene that you might want to photograph in the future and shoot it using a 1 second or longer exposure, with the Long Exposure NR feature on and then off. Do the same at a faster shutter speed while using ISO 1600 and then ISO 3200 with High ISO NR on and then off. Examine the images at 100% magnification on your computer monitor. You should be able to quickly decide whether you prefer the smoother effect provided by each of the NR features or the sharper effect—with better resolution but a grainy look—when the NR feature is off.

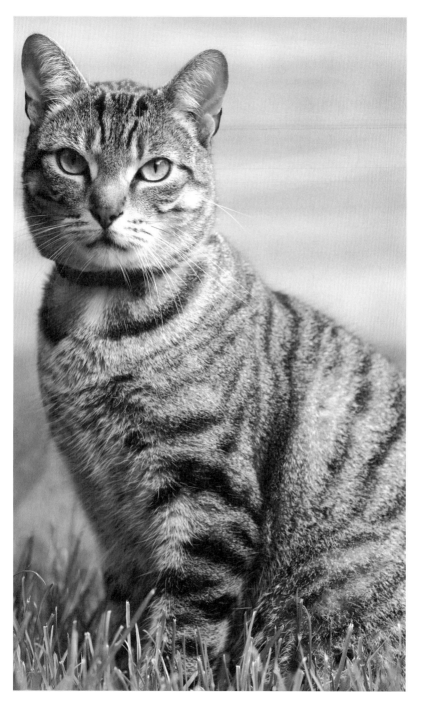

The Menus

Many of the features discussed in the previous chapter are accessible with analog controls or by pressing the [Fn] button, a camera design that reduces the amount of time needed for hunting and pecking through a multi-page menu. As a result, the ∝200 has fewer menu options than some other D-SLRs, but it still offers an extensive list.

To access the ∝200's electronic menus, press [MENU] (located on back of camera to left of LCD monitor). A series of tabs identifies each of the pages; scroll to the one you want with the left/right keys of the Controller. Then, scroll up or down on any page with the Controller keys or the camera's Control dial [dial icon].

The rest of the menu navigation is also straightforward. When you reach an item of interest, press the button (marked AF) in the center of the Controller. That will reveal the options available for that Menu item, such as [On] and [Off], or other choices. Scroll to the one you want to set and press the center button to confirm your selection. That final step also returns you to the full menu screen.

Note: You will be utilizing the AF button in the middle of the Controller quite often to confirm selections when working with the menu system. I will refer to it throughout this chapter as the center button; think of this as an "OK" button.

↻ *The ∝200 includes a wide range of features in its electronic menu, each discussed in this chapter with recommendations as to which might be the most useful for helping you get them most from your camera.*

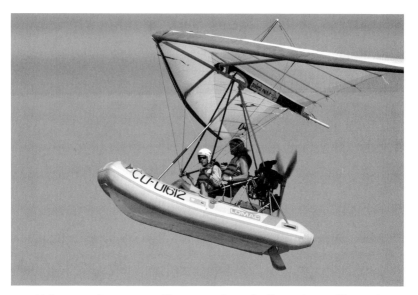

Unless you have a specific reason for selecting a lower Size and Quality level when shooting JPEGs, it's worth using the highest level for each to get the best possible results. When you need much smaller JPEGs for Web use or for making small prints, simply downsize the file with image editing software.

There are several distinct menus, each with their own set of tabs (denoting individual pages or screens): Recording Menu 1 and 2 📷 , Custom Menu 1 ✿ , Playback Menu 1 and 2 ► and Setup Menu 1, 2, and 3 ✎ .

The Recording Menus 📷

These let you define image parameters such as size, quality, and format. They are also used to control flash, noise reduction, the creative styles, etc.

Recording Menu 1 📷 1
Access this screen for the following items:

[Image size]: For JPEGs, select [L:10M] for 10-megapixel resolution (Large, or 3872 x 2592 pixels), [M:5.6M] for 5-

megapixel resolution (Medium, or 2256 x 1496 pixels), or [S:2.5M] for 2.5-megapixel resolution (Small, or 1920 x 1280 pixels). These sizes are discussed in detail on pages 52-54. Press the center button not only to confirm your selection, but also to return to the menu screen.

[Aspect Ratio]: Select the standard [3:2] aspect ratio (the default), or choose the longer/narrower [16:9] format. The latter is intended primarily for producing an image proportion or shape that's ideal for viewing on a wide-screen TV monitor, as discussed on page 57.

[Quality]: Four options are available for making images. When recording in the RAW format, options include [RAW] and [RAW+J] (RAW & JPEG simultaneously). When recoding JPEGs, you can select either [FINE] (lower compression/ larger file size) or [STD] (Standard—higher compression/ smaller file size). See pages 54-57 for a description of how and why you might want to use any of these options.

Note: When you select [RAW] or [RAW+J], the camera automatically sets image size to the highest megapixel level; that depends on the Aspect Ratio that you have set. The JPEG quality is also automatically set to [Fine]. Now, the item for [Image size] in the Menu is blacked out, so it cannot be accessed. I often use RAW format because of the superior image-enhancing options available in conversion software for this format. Shooting a JPEG file at the same time can be useful if you own image-browser software that does not recognize the Sony ARW format files; at least you can view the JPEG file.

[Creative Style]: A feature discussed at length on pages 70-72, this item allows you to modify the look of the images, with styles such as [Vivid] [Vivid]†, [Portrait] [Portrait]†, [Landscape] [Landscape]†, and others. It also allows for increasing or decreasing the level of contrast, color saturation, and sharpness within each of the style options.

[Flash control]: The default setting is [ADI flash] (it stands for Advanced Distance Integration), the most sophisticated option for light metering when flash is used. It is only available when using Sony lenses, Carl Zeiss ZA (Alpha) lenses, or D-series Konica Minolta Maxxum/Dynax lenses. It will operate with the built-in flash, with Sony HV series flash units, and with Maxxum/Dynax D-series flash units. When a compatible lens and the built-in flash or ADI compatible accessory flash are used, the camera's flash exposure metering system considers data about subject distance in its calculation process.

If you are using other lenses or an older Konica Minolta flash unit, the camera will automatically switch to Pre-flash TTL metering to compensate for the lack of distance information. You can also select the [Pre-flash TTL] option, described in more detail in the chapter on flash (see page 155), but I see no reason for doing so in normal shooting. Sony does recommend that you use Pre-flash TTL instead of ADI flash in certain specific situations, such as when using flash with a polarizer on your lens or a wide-angle diffuser attached to the flash unit.

[Flash Compens.] ⚡ : After scrolling to this item for setting flash compensation, press the center button of the Controller (AF) to produce a scale in the LCD that allows you to increase flash intensity (scrolling toward a + setting) or to decrease flash intensity (scrolling toward a – setting). By default, the pointer is at zero. You can scroll with the Controller keys or the camera's Control dial to any point from -2 (for a major reduction in flash output) to +2 (for a significant increase in flash output.) This is a useful feature for producing subtle flash lighting or for increasing intensity in situations where the subject is not adequately bright; this technique will be discussed in the Flash chapter.

Recording Menu 2 ☐ 2

Items available on this menu page are:

[Priority setup]: The first option, [AF], is the default setting. It ensures the camera will not take a photo unless focus has been confirmed. You can also select [Release], which allows the camera to fire whether focus is confirmed or not. Some photographers may want to use the [Release] option for taking candid pictures in low light, preferring to get a slightly out-of-focus image to no image at all. Remember to reset your priority to [AF] afterwards; that will minimize the number of out-of-focus pictures that you will take.

[AF illuminator]: The default setting for this item is [On]. When the built-in flash is up, it will fire several short bursts in low light to assist the AF system in acquiring focus. You can turn this feature [Off] if your friends find the multiple bursts of light annoying while you're taking their pictures. The AF system should still be reliable except in very dark conditions.

[Long exp. NR]: When this option for long exposure noise reduction is set to its default [On], the camera automatically provides additional noise reduction processing for images made at a shutter speed of 1 second or longer. That minimizes the visibility of the digital noise pattern, as discussed on page 79. You can set it to [Off] if you prefer a more grainy effect.

[High ISO NR]: This item is [On] by default so the camera will provide extra noise reduction processing at ISO 1600 to ISO 3200 to minimize the visibility of the digital noise pattern as discussed on page 79. You can set it to [Off].

[Rec mode reset]: If you want to re-set many of the camera's features to the factory programmed defaults, select this item and press the center button to confirm your decision. (Note that a [Reset Default] item is also available in the [Setup Menu 3 ⚒ 3] as discussed on page 99; that option provides the same effect but it also resets two additional camera features.) Resetting can be useful after extensive experimentation with various ∝200 controls and menu items.

The Custom Menus ✿

Sony has provided a wide range of options for customizing camera operation to meet personal preferences and these are listed under this tab. Scroll to any desired item, press the center button, scroll to the desired option and press the center button again to confirm your decision.

Custom Menu 1 ✿ 1

This menu includes only a single page, listing items that you can activate or de-activate to meet personal preference.

[Eye-Start AF]: By default, this feature is on, so the ∝200 will automatically activate autofocus and its other systems when it detects your eye at the viewfinder. Of course, the camera will activate those items whenever anything blocks the viewfinder, such as your hand or leg while carrying the ∝200; that inadvertent activation can cause needless battery drain. Should that be problematic, you will want to turn Eye-Start Off with this custom item.

[AEL button]: This controls the function of the camera's AE lock button. (AE lock is a feature used to lock an exposure value before recomposing, as discussed on page 133.) Two options are available. When [AEL hold] (the default) is set, the AEL button is active only while you depress it. If you do not maintain pressure on the AEL button, the exposure value will not remain locked.

The other option, [AEL toggle], provides an on/off effect. Press the AEL button once and exposure value is locked. It remains locked; there is no need to keep it depressed while you recompose a scene. To turn AE lock off, press the button again. The selection of [AEL toggle] might be useful in landscape photography to lock the exposure values while you recompose the shot; you won't need to keep the AEL button pressed continuously. However, it can also lead to serious exposure errors if you forget that this option has been set and then forget to toggle AE lock off when switching to a different subject, or when the light level changes. (Naturally,

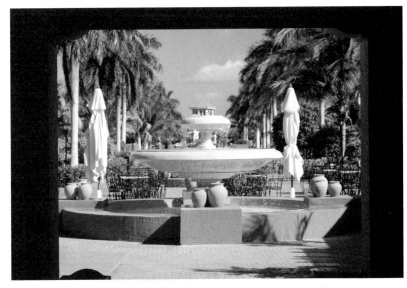

When you're shooting situations that do not require the camera to set focus and exposure instantly, there's really no need to keep the the Eye-Start feature on. Reserve that amenity for photo opportunities that really benefit from instant response, such as candid people pictures.

AEL is automatically disengaged when the camera goes into power-saving sleep mode.)

[Ctrl dial setup]: This item allows you to change the function of the Control dial, but only in the camera's P (Program) and M (Manual) exposure modes. The [Shutter speed] option is the camera's default setting. When you rotate the dial the shutter speed will change. (In P mode, the camera will then automatically set an appropriate aperture or f/stop.) When using the M mode, you can also change the aperture at any time but you must press and hold the exposure compensation button ![+/-] while rotating the Control dial. The [Aperture] option allows you to use the Control dial to select a desired aperture (f/stop) instead. (In P mode, the camera will then automatically set the appropriate shutter speed.) When using the M mode, you can also change the shutter speed at any time but you must press and hold the exposure compensation button ⊞ while rotating the Control dial.

[Red eye reduc.]: When set to [On], this feature ensures that red-eye reduction is always active when the flash is used. The camera will rapidly fire several bright bursts before the actual flash exposure. That feature can be disengaged by selecting [Off], which is the camera's default setting.

[Auto review]: After you take a photo, instant playback, or automatic review, is provided for 5 seconds by default; this allows for quickly checking the photo without consuming a lot of battery power. You can change that instant playback time to [Off] (no auto review will be provided), or to [5 seconds] (my preferred setting), or to [10 seconds]. Remember, you can examine any image for longer periods of time by using the camera's Playback mode.

[Auto off w/ VF]: By default, this item is [On], so the camera's LCD screen blacks out as a power saving measure whenever you use the viewfinder. This is a logical setting, but you can also select [Off], forcing the LCD screen to remain active at all times, which can consume unnecessary battery power.

Playback Menus ▶

Playback allows you to review your images in the LCD monitor after you have recorded them. This often helps you determine whether you need to reshoot a particular picture or not. Two distinct menus are available to provide selection for items that are relevant to Playback operation in the camera.

Playback Menu 1 ▶ 1

[Delete]: This setting erases images from your memory card, either images that you mark for deletion, or all images on the card. Caution is urged when you use this option because

90

images deleted cannot normally be recovered, except with special aftermarket software.

If you select the [Marked images] option, you can specify the images to be deleted. This choice displays images on your memory card as thumbnails. Scroll through them using the left/right Controller keys and select frames for deletion by pressing the Controller's center (AF) button. A trashcan symbol ⅲ will appear to confirm your selection. If you accidentally select a frame for deletion, you can deselect it by again pressing the center button; the ⅲ will disappear. After you finish marking images for deletion, press the MENU button, scroll up to [Delete], and press the central AF button to confirm deletion of the marked images.

[Format]: This item re-formats the memory card, permanently erasing all data. Even protected images are deleted. When [Format] is highlighted, press the center (AF) button and choose [OK] from the confirmation screen. Verify your decision by again pressing the center button, and a final screen will confirm the formatting activity. Be sure that you are ready to delete all images; even the best aftermarket recovery software may not be able to recover any or all images after a card is formatted.

Note: Never remove a memory card when formatting is underway; it could damage your card. I recommend reformatting the card every time after you download images to your computer's hard drive or other backup system to keep the card performing at its optimum level. This formatting should always be done in-camera, and not using a formatting option available in a computer because the latter may not properly format the card.

[Protect]: This selection allows you to mark images so that they cannot be accidentally deleted. Use the Controller keys to first scroll right and then up/down to select [Marked images.] This option displays images on your memory card as thumbnails. Scroll through them using the left/right Controller keys and select frames for protection by pressing the

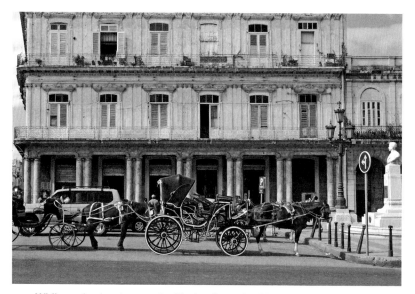

While reviewing images in Playback mode, it's worth marking your favorites for protection. This will ensure that they cannot be inadvertently erased with the camera's delete command. They can be deleted only by formatting the memory card.

center button on the Controller; a key symbol 🔑 will appear to confirm that the image is locked. Any such images will not be inadvertently deleted, even if you use the camera's [Delete all] feature. However, formatting the memory card will delete even the protected images.

If you accidentally select a frame for protection, you can deselect it by again pressing the center button; the key 🔑 will disappear. After you finish marking images for protection, press the MENU button, scroll to the OK option and press the center button of the Controller to start the protection process.

Two other options are available: [All images] will quickly apply the protection, or lock, to every photo that is currently on the memory card. [Cancel all] will remove the lock from every image that you had previously marked for protection.

[DPOF setup]: This option designates files on your memory card for direct printing using a DPOF (Digital Print Order Format) compliant printer.

The three choices for [DPOF setup] are selected in a similar way as the same options in the Delete and Protect menus:

[Marked images] lets you choose one or more files for DPOF. Only JPEGs can be marked for printing. Scroll through the thumbnails and enter those for DPOF by pressing the center button; "DPOF1" will appear under the images that you mark, indicating that you want one print of that image. If you want more than one print of that image, press the center button as often as you wish, and the DPOF number will increase. Then, use the left/right keys of the Controller to scroll to another image that you want to mark. When you're finished marking images for DPOF printing, press the MENU button.

If you choose the [All images] option, a screen will appear allowing you to set the number of prints that will be made of each photo. Select the number by scrolling up and down. When you're finished, press the center button, scroll to [OK], and press the center button again to confirm your selection.

[Date imprint]: When set to [On], the date will be printed on the photo when DPOF printing is used with compatible DPOF compliant printers. The date is not printed on the actual JPEG image file, only on the print.

[Index print]: The [On] option creates an index of thumbnail prints for all images in a folder for subsequent printing with a DPOF compliant printer. The number of images printed per sheet varies from printer to printer. Highlight [Off] to cancel the index print. Press the center button to confirm your selection.

Playback Menu 2 ▶ 2

This menu page provides only a few options:

By default, the camera is set to rotate images made in a vertical orientation so they fill the entire LCD monitor. Therefore, vertical images will appear sideways in the LCD so they fill the entire screen. That applies to images viewed in instant or full Playback. If you do not want vertical images to be rotated automatically, select the [Manual rotate] option in this menu item. Now, any vertical image will appear vertically in the LCD, making it smaller in the screen, since it will not be rotated automatically. If you want to manually rotate a particular image, you can do so by pressing the Fn button while viewing a photo.

[Slide show]: Press the center (AF) button after scrolling to this item and a slide show of all images on the memory card will begin on your LCD monitor. The display will show one image every three seconds. To pause and restart the slide show, press the center button again. To move ahead or go back quickly, press the left/right Controller keys. To cancel the slide show, press the MENU button.

[Interval]: This item allows you to change the period of time that each image will be displayed during a slide show to 1, 5, 10, or 30 seconds. Unless your images are really stunning, a 3 second interval is usually just right.

Setup Menus ✎

Use the Setup menus to establish or change certain aspects of camera operation to meet your own specifications. Three distinct screens are available under the Setup tab, each with its own list of items.

Setup Menu 1 ✎ 1

This page offers a list of six items that you might occasionally want to access.

[LCD brightness]: Pressing the center button in the Controller reveals a scale. Scroll to the right (toward the plus side) to make the LCD display brighter, to the extent that you want. Scroll to the left (toward the minus side) to make the display darker.

The higher you set the monitor brightness level, the easier it is to see data or images on the LCD monitor in bright conditions. However, setting the brightness higher or lower than the default makes it more difficult to correctly evaluate exposure (actual image brightness) on the LCD monitor.

[Info disp time]: One of the benefits of the ∝200 is that all shooting data is displayed on the large LCD monitor instead of a small secondary data panel, as with many competing cameras. (If the data is not appearing while the camera is in capture mode, press the DISP button or remove any object that is near the viewfinder.) By default, the data is displayed for only 5 seconds before the LCD screen goes dark to save battery power. That's not very long so it can be extended with this menu item to 10 seconds, 30 seconds, or a full 1 minute. The longer intervals are fine when you have a spare battery, but the default setting is preferable in other cases. (The same recommendation applies to the next items in this menu and to the Auto Review item in ✿ 1 discussed earlier in this chapter.)

[Power save]: By default, the ∝200 will go into power saving Sleep mode in one minute when the camera is not used at all. You can change this time to one of several other options from 3 minutes to 30 minutes. A very long time will increase battery consumption, so choose such an option only for a specific reason.

[Video output]: You must select a TV/broadcast standard if you want to play back images on a TV set. Two options are available for video system compatibility: [NTSC] (North American standard also used in Japan, the default) and [PAL] (Europe and many other countries). Make enquiries as to which standard to use in your geographic area.

[Language]: This item allows you to set a preferred language for all text that is displayed in the LCD screen, including all menu items. Press the center button and scroll up/down until you reach your preferred language; then press the center button again to confirm your decision.

[Date/Time setup]: Set the date and time when you first get your ∝200, and change them when needed. A screen will display a field for Year/Month/Day; you can modify the data in any of the three fields by scrolling up and down. Fields are also provided for the Hour/Minute/PM or AM, and you can scroll until the correct data appears in each of these fields. This data will not be printed on your images, but it will be recorded for every image and can later be accessed with image editing software.

If you are not happy with the Year/Month/Day format, keep scrolling to the right until the cursor reaches the field at the bottom right corner of the screen. Now, scrolling up/down allows you to change the format for the data to Month/Day/Year or to Day/Month/Year, if you prefer one of those alternatives. Press the center button after you complete all entries for date/time setup.

Setup Menu 2 ⚲ 2

[File number]: This menu function manages how the camera will label images in different folders on the memory card. The default setting is [Series]. Each time you take a new photo, the file number will be one greater than the number for the previously saved file until 9999 is reached. (That is a logical procedure.)

If you select the [Reset] option, the file numbering will be reset to 0001 when the folder format is changed and when all images in a folder are deleted, whenever you switch to a new memory card, and when you format a memory card. Use this option only if you have a specific reason for doing so. If you select [Reset], the file numbering will restart at 0001 quite often; hence, you will eventually have many images with the same file number. The [Series] option ensures that this will not happen, at least not until after you have taken 9,999 photos with your camera.

96

[Folder name]: This option is used to determine which of two formats are assigned to name folders on the memory card. Each consists of eight characters. [Standard form] (the default) creates a label for folders such as 100MSDCF. You may prefer to select [Date form], a format that follows a sequence such as 10090222, which is the folder number plus the year, month, and day. Thus the example above indicates a folder created on Feb. 22, 2009. If you select the [Date form] option, a new folder will be created on each day when you make an image with the camera; this is very convenient. All images made that day will be saved in that folder.

[New folder]: Use this item to create new folders on your memory card. From [Select folder], scroll down to highlight [New folder], then right to highlight [Enter]. Press the center button to create a new folder that will use the format currently in use for Folder name (described above). Every time you create a new folder, the folder number increases automatically by one greater than the previous folder on the memory card.

[Select folder]: This item allows you to specify the folder to which subsequent images should be saved. When you select this item, you'll see a list of current file folders that have been created. Specify the one that you want to use to store the next set of images that you will shoot. Do note, however, that this option is available only when the Standard format is being used; it cannot be selected when folders are named in the Date format.

[USB connection]: The default setting is [Mass Storage], which allows a computer to recognize the camera as a USB mass storage device. That is useful if you will be attaching the camera directly to a computer via a USB cable in order to download your images. Select [PTP] for making prints directly from the camera using a PictBridge compatible printer. This will require connecting the ∝200 to the printer using the USB cable.

[Audio signals]: The default setting is [On], which causes the camera to beep when focus is confirmed in Autofocus mode. Select Off to disable this audio feature.

Setup Menu 3 ⌁ 3

Only two items are provided in this screen: for sensor cleaning and camera resetting.

[Cleaning mode]: Even though the ∝200 possesses an internal anti-dust feature, debris may still accumulate on your sensor from time to time. Use this menu item to gain access to the CCD sensor if you notice dust specks in your photos. A fully charged battery or the optional AC adapter is required. Proceed at your own risk! If you choose to use this process, follow these steps:

1. After selecting the Cleaning mode item, press the central AF button and scroll up to highlight [OK].

2. A note will then appear in the LCD monitor informing you to shut the camera off after the cleaning is finished.

3. After you click on OK (with the center button), the camera's reflex mirror is raised to reveal the sensor.

4. Remove the lens or body cap.

5. Hold the camera facing downward and pump a blast of air from a large blower bulb toward the sensor; repeat this a couple of times to dislodge any dust particles. Use extreme care not to touch anything inside the camera's mirror box. (Should the camera begin beeping during this time, turn it off immediately; the beep is a warning about inadequate battery power.)

6. After cleaning is finished, replace the lens, or body cap and turn the camera off. The reflex mirror will return to its normal position.

Caution: Proceed at your own risk. Improper cleaning may damage the CCD sensor and require expensive repair. Use extreme care when the CCD sensor is exposed. Use a large blower brush (sold by photo retailers) to produce a puff of air to blow away specks. Do not use a can of compressed air because propellant may be sprayed and that can damage the CCD. Sony does not recommend the use of sensor cleaning kits (swabs or brushes and liquids) that are marketed by third-party manufacturers such as Photosol and VisibleDust. Contact a Sony authorized service center for professional cleaning if you have trouble removing dust.

[Reset default]: This control returns all of the camera features to the factory-set defaults. That includes exposure compensation, metering mode, AF mode, Drive mode, WB, Creative Style, Noise Reduction, and so on. It's useful after you have been experimenting with many of the camera's many features. A Reset function is also available in Recording Menu 2 📷 2 as well (discussed earlier in this chapter); that provides almost the identical results with two exceptions: This [Reset default] in the Setup Menu resets two additional items. In Playback mode, the camera will display a single image with recording data displayed; when the camera is used in recording mode, the enlarged data screen will be displayed (instead of the more detailed data screen in smaller font).

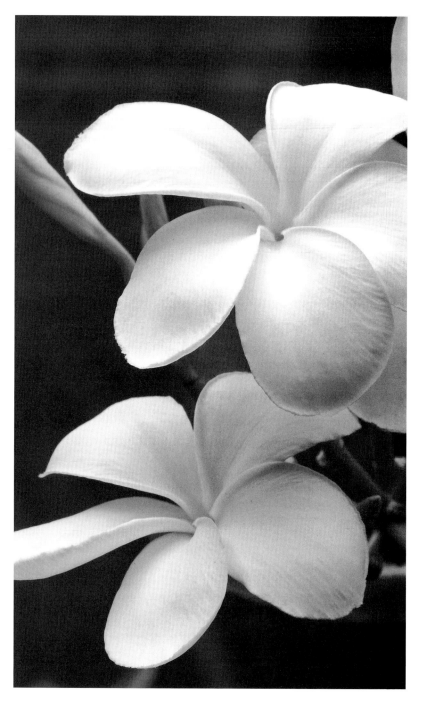

Camera and Shooting Operations

Image Sharpness

Various factors contribute to the sharpness of an image. While focus, depth-of-field, and even use of flash play a role, proper handholding technique is also essential. If you don't use proper technique, camera movement may degrade image sharpness and your pictures will be disappointing. A good way to evaluate your technique is to review your photos. If the focused subject is not crisp, but another element in the scene is sharp, the problem is usually caused by an improperly focused image. However, if nothing in the photo is tack sharp, the cause is probably camera movement.

Long lenses, especially, are often heavy and difficult to hold steady. Just as telephotos magnify the subject, longer lenses magnify the effect of any camera movement. A rule of thumb suggests that your shutter speed should approximate the reciprocal of the effective focal length of the lens in use to make sharp photos. For example, a 100mm equivalent lens would require a hand-held shutter speed of about 1/125 second, while 500mm equivalent would require at least 1/500 second. (When considering this, remember that due to the size of its sensor, the 35mm equivalent focal length of a lens on the ∝200 is the actual focal length multiplied by 1.5) If you cannot achieve a high enough shutter speed at your desired aperture setting, you can increase your ISO, but beware of digital noise at ISO 1600 and especially at higher ISO levels. If you want to shoot at long shutter speeds, use a tripod or other camera support.

The A200 is equipped with valuable features that help provide optimal image quality, such as the Super SteadyShot system used for this photo, made at a shutter speed of 1/60 second using a telephoto zoom lens at a 200mm focal length.

Handholding Technique

Proper technique will maximize the odds of a sharp photo when handholding the camera. Hold the camera's grip in your right hand with your index finger on the shutter button. For horizontal (landscape format) pictures, cradle the lens and body in your left hand so that your fingers can comfortably operate the lens if necessary. For vertical (portrait format) shots, turn the camera so your right hand is on top and the opposite end of the camera is cradled in your left hand. With either format, keep your elbows in, pressed gently against your body for additional support. Spread you legs apart in a firm, but comfortable, stance. When you are ready to take a picture, exhale and roll your finger across the shutter button, making sure to hold the camera level.

The Super SteadyShot (SSS) System ⟪👋⟫

Sony has incorporated an improved version of its anti-shake technology into the ∝200. Unlike some other manufacturers' stabilization systems, which work by shifting elements within a lens, Super SteadyShot shifts the sensor inside the camera body. This provides image stabilization with virtually all Maxxum/Dynax lenses, all Sony lenses, and the Carl Zeiss ZA series marketed by Sony. It should also work with aftermarket brand lenses with the appropriate mount.

Turn the anti-shake feature on with the Super SteadyShot switch ⟪👋⟫ . The system consists of a sensor that detects motion and a mechanical device. When the in-camera sensor detects motion, a microcomputer analyzes data on focal length, aperture setting, and focusing distance and sends a signal to a motor which mechanically shifts the entire CCD sensor unit to compensate. The incoming light rays are refracted and the projected image is returned to the center of the frame, which produces a sharper image.

The SSS feature is designed primarily for hand-held use at shutter speeds shorter than 1/4 second. When the system is active, a scale ▪▃▅ is displayed on the right side of the viewfinder data panel, featuring five distinct bars. During stabilizer operation, one or more bars will be illuminated. Whenever all five bars are visible, there is a high risk that the image will be blurred to some extent by camera shake.

Note: The Super SteadyShot stabilizer is not fully active when the camera is first turned on or when it first wakes from power-saving Sleep mode. Initially, five bars are illuminated indicating that the system is not yet fully effective. After about one second, you may find that fewer bars are visible; that confirms full stabilizer effectiveness. In low light, when using a long shutter speed, all five bars may be continuously illumi- nated; that is a warning that the system is working to its maxi- mum ability. In bright light, the scale may not appear at all; that is an indicator that the shutter speed in use is adequately fast, requiring no image stabilization activity.

When the ∝200 is set to an operating mode that allows the camera to set the shutter speed, another icon may occasionally appear in the viewfinder data panel. This is a warning that the stabilizer is working at maximum effectiveness but blurring from camera shake is likely due to a long shutter speed or the use of a long focal length lens. (That icon will not appear when the camera is set to the Manual or Shutter in Priority (S) mode, or when you have shifted the shutter speed while using the Program (P) mode.) Should you receive that warning, consider using a faster shutter speed to make the shot, or brace the camera against something solid for additional support to increase the odds of making a sharp photo.

SSS in Use
Sony indicates that the SSS system should allow you to handhold the camera at 2.5 to 3.5 shutter-speed steps longer than the rule of thumb suggests. Take a conservative approach to be sure of getting photos without blurring from camera shake. Stay within two steps of your normal mini- mum hand-holdable shutter speed. Use even faster shutter speeds if practical, especially if maximum SteadyShot activ- ity is denoted by five bars in the SSS indicator scale. You

may decide to exceed this recommendation, using even longer shutter speeds, especially if you're particularly steady when handholding any lens or if faced with an "all or nothing" shooting situation.

With large, heavy telephoto lenses, use a tripod. Sony recommends you disengage the SSS system whenever you use a tripod. (The SSS system was not designed for effectiveness when a tripod is used.) When shooting from an unstable platform, such as a boat, activate the SSS system and use fast shutter speeds: at least 1/60 second with a 28mm focal length and at least 1/500 second at the 300mm end of a zoom lens.

Note: Be aware that Super SteadyShot use increases power drain by roughly 30%, so take an extra battery if you plan on using it a lot during a very long day of shooting.

The Focusing System

The ∝200 is equipped with a sophisticated TTL phase-detection autofocus (AF) system to assure quick, accurate focusing in almost all picture-taking situations. It utilizes eight line-type CCD focus detection points plus a center cross-hatched point. The location and angle of each focus detection point—called Focus Area by Sony—is denoted on the viewfinder screen. The central point is the most sensitive because it reads both vertical and horizontal patterns.

The AF system functions in light that is the ISO 100 equivalent of 0 EV to 18 EV (from low light to very bright conditions). There is also an AF illuminator feature, available with the built-in flash and accessory flash units; this helps the camera to focus in low light when using flash. However, the ∝200 provides reliable autofocus in surprisingly dark conditions even without that focus-assist feature.

The autofocus system is very effective in most situations and with *most types of subject matter. For action photography, be sure to switch to Continuous Autofocus (AF-C); the system will then activate full time "tracking" focus, increasing the odds of sharp images.*

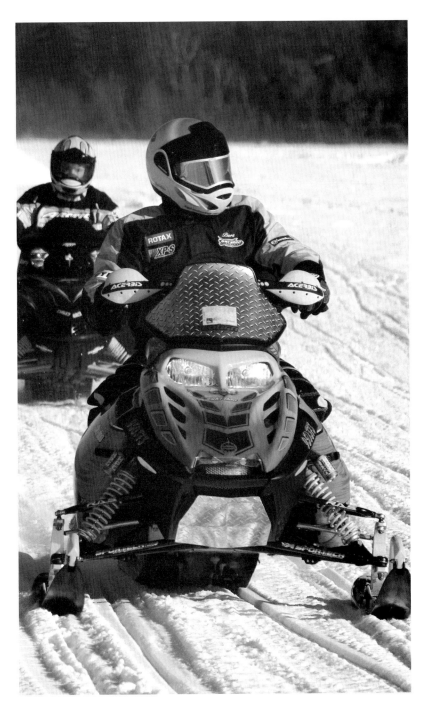

Three options define how the focus detection points (or AF areas) are used by the system: Wide AF area, Spot AF area, or Local area selection. The camera also offers three AF modes: Single-shot AF (AF-S), Automatic AF (AF-A), and Continuous AF (AF-C). You can also operate the ∝200 using fully manual focus.

AF Modes

To set autofocus, flip the AF/MF switch (located on left side of camera, below the lens release button) to the AF position. Then press the **Fn** button to access the [Autofocus mode] sub-menu; scroll to any of the three AF mode options and select the one you want by pressing the Controller's central button.

Single-Shot AF **AF-S** : This mode is intended for static subjects. Activate autofocus with a touch of the shutter release button. (If Eye-Control is on, the camera will activate AF as soon as you look through the viewfinder.) During autofocus operation, the **(())** symbol will appear in the viewfinder data panel. When focus is acquired, the focus detection point that found focus will light in red on the viewing screen; the focus confirmation signal **●** will appear as a solid green dot. As long as slight pressure is maintained on the shutter button, focus remains locked; you can now recompose without changing focus.

Note: When you use focus lock with the camera set to Multi Segment metering, exposure is also locked. That allows for optimizing both focus and exposure for your primary subject. Should you switch to one of the other metering patterns, exposure will not be locked automatically when focus is locked; you would need to use the AEL button as discussed on page 133.

Continuous AF **AF-C** : This mode activates full-time tracking focus. Focus is never locked, but shifts continuously as the camera-to-subject distance changes. Focus lock is not available; if you recompose, focus will change. (Some Maxxum/Dynax and Sony telephoto lenses incorporate a focus hold button that allows you to lock focus in AF-C mode.) The active AF area that finds focus will be illuminated in the viewfinder; a (⊚) symbol will also appear confirming focus. If focus cannot be acquired, the camera will not allow you to take a photo; the focus indicator (❨❩) will blink in the viewfinder data panel. When AF-C is selected, the flash unit's focus-assist feature will not operate.

AF-C is ideal for action photography because tracking focus starts instantly without the delay that occurs in AF-A mode when the camera must switch between AF-S and AF-C. The system is most reliable (virtually foolproof) in brightly lit outdoor photography. Like any AF system, it's not quite as fast in very low light.

If the camera cannot find focus, the focus signal ● will blink in the viewfinder data panel. You cannot take a picture until focus is confirmed unless you have set the [Release] option under [Priority Setup] in [Recording Menu 2 📷 2] (see page 87).

Automatic AF AF-A : In this mode, the AF system switches automatically from Single-shot AF to Continuous AF mode if the system detects subject motion. This is the camera's default mode and it's recommended for multi-purpose use. With static subjects, AF-A mode works exactly like AF-S mode.

When subject motion is detected, the system switches to using AF-C mode in order to track the subject's progress. This AF-A option is particularly useful for subjects that are static but might begin to move soon. Response to motion may take a second or two as the AF system adjusts for the changing camera-to-subject distance. Hence, the first shot or two in a series may not be perfectly focused.

AF Area Selection
The ∝200 can employ nine focus detection points—called AF areas by Sony—in order to find focus. You can select any of three distinct focus point options by pressing the Fn button and selecting the [AF area] sub menu. You can then scroll to any of the following three options; select the one you want by pressing the Controller's central button.

Wide AF area ⌞ ⌟ **:** This is the camera's default mode. All of the system's focus points are active and the camera uses automated focus point selection. Focusing is completed when one or more of the nine points finds focus. The active focus point (or points, when the scene includes several objects at the same distance from the camera) are then illuminated in red on the viewing screen.

The automated system cannot read your mind, so it will not always use the focus detection point that covers your primary subject. In a scene with several objects, the system may select the closest subject or the object with the greatest contrast or most distinct texture. With "difficult" subjects—those with unusual patterns, for example—the central focus point (or AF area) will often set focus so that the object in the center of the frame will be sharpest. This is because the central focus point is cross-hatched—it includes both horizontal and vertical sensors and is capable of acquiring focus even with subjects that may hinder the other focus detection points.

The Wide AF area option, with its automated focus point selection, is often used for action photography because it can focus on off-center subjects. It also works well for snapshots or point-and-shoot photography. Naturally, the system will not always produce the intended effect, possibly focusing on a secondary element that's closer to the camera or is a more reliable target than your preferred subject.

Note: While using the Wide AF area, you can switch at any time to using only the central focus detection point—called "Spot Focus." Simply press the AF button in the center of the Controller and the camera will instantly focus using only the central point. After you release the button, it will automatically revert to the standard wide area AF approach. This feature is useful in a situation described above, where the AF sytem sets focus on a secondary element instead of your primary subject.

Spot AF area ⠿ : When you select this option, the ∝200 will employ only the central focus detection point; the other eight points will not be active. Target your subject and lock focus by keeping the shutter button pressed halfway while recomposing. The central focus detection point (Spot-AF area) is more reliable in low-light photography than any of the other points. As well, Spot AF area is useful in action photography—when the subject is large or located in the center of the frame—in combination with the AF-C mode. Because the central focus detection point is the most sensitive, it is the most reliable in quickly focusing on an approaching subject, such as a galloping horse or a race car.

Local ⦿ : In this mode, you can select any of the nine focus detection points—or local AF areas—and you can change the active point at any time. Use the Controller keys to select one of the outside focus areas while looking at an off-center subject through the viewfinder. Once a focus point is selected, it will be briefly illuminated in red on the viewing screen when it finds focus. To quickly select the central focus point (Spot AF area), press the AF button in the center of the Controller.

The ability to manually select any of the several focus detection points is common to many brands of D-SLRs. This feature certainly sounds useful and logical. However, unless I'm shooting an action subject that may drift off-center, I generally use only the central focus area, often with focus lock. Nevertheless, you may find circumstances where you'll want to select one of the other eight "local" focus area points, and that option is certainly available to you.

Manual Focus

To use manual focus, set the AF/MF switch to the MF position. This disengages the autofocus system so you can focus manually at any time using the focus ring on your lens. (Manual focus is not available when using any of the six Scene modes discussed later in this chapter; the camera will always use autofocus.) If you are having trouble focusing in dark locations, or you want to set focus in anticipation of an event, you can estimate the subject distance and set the focus accordingly. (Of course, this works only with lenses that include a focus distance scale.)

When focus is acquired, the focus signal in the data panel confirms focus by lighting steadily ● . However, when focusing manually, you can take a picture anytime, even if focus is not confirmed.

I recommend switching to MF occasionally, especially in macro, landscape, and architectural photography, when you may want to set the point of focus in the scene to control depth of field. The manual focus option is also ideal for critical focus on a small, specific subject element: the eyes in a portrait or the stamen in the heart of a blossom, for examples. Finally, it's a convenient method for focusing on one segment of a scene while setting exposure for an entirely different area.

Drive Modes

The function of the drive modes is similar to that performed by the motor drive in a film camera. While no film has to be transported, these modes control the firing and recocking of the camera's shutter mechanism.

Set the drive mode by pressing the Drive mode button ⟲/⎗ (on the camera's right "shoulder"). Use the Controller keys to scroll to a desired option and confirm your selection by pressing the central button.

Single-shot adv. ☐
The ∝200's default drive, this selection will cause the camera to take one photo each time you press the shutter button. Select this option when you simply want to shoot one image at a time rather than in a bracket or a burst.

Continuous adv. ⎗
In Continuous Advance, the camera will keep recording images as long as the shutter button is held down. If you are

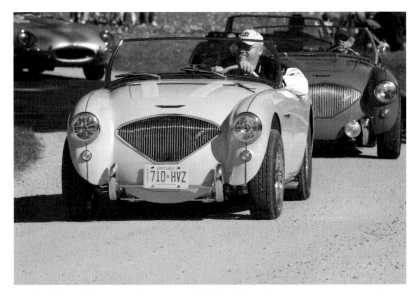

The Continuous advance mode is ideal whenever you want to shoot a series of several photos in quick succession. In action photography, combine this mode with Continuous Autofocus for the best results.

using a high-speed memory card and shooting JPEGs, the camera will fire until the card is full. (With slower cards or when using RAW capture mode, the number of frames-per-burst will be limited.) This is useful when you want to shoot a series of images, whether friends being silly or action at a sports event. It will shoot at a rate of up to 3 frames per second (fps) as long as the shutter speed is 1/250 second or faster. If longer shutter speeds are used, the framing rate will be slower.

Note: The framing rate can be quite slow when flash is used because the flash must recycle after each image in order to fire again. The recycle time depends on the amount of flash output used when making an image. There's a long recycle time when high output is required (great flash-to-subject distances), and a quick recycle time when lower output is required (with nearby subjects or in bright light).

10sec self-timer ⏱10

When this option is selected, the camera waits 10 seconds after the shutter button is pressed before it fires. This can be useful when the photographer wants to get into the picture and when the camera is mounted on a tripod. Focus and exposure are set when you first press the shutter button. If the lighting changes during the 10-second delay, the exposure may not be correct.

2sec self-timer ⏱ 2

Selected by scrolling to the right from the [⏱10] item, this option provides only a two-second delay between pressing the shutter and when the shutter actually fires. This option may be used for tripping the shutter when using long shutter speeds, or telephoto or macro lenses, while the camera is on a tripod. This way a photo can be taken without touching the camera and creating vibration. Focus and exposure are set when you first press the shutter button, so it is best used with fairly static subjects.

Hint: If you photograph birds or animals, it's best to use one of the optional remote control accessories, RM-S1AM (short) or RM-L1AM (long), instead of using the self-timer. This will allow you to trip the shutter at exactly the right instant without jarring the camera. (The 2-second self-timer is not often practical with moving subjects.)

Note: In addition to the familiar drive modes above, the Drive mode button also provides Exposure Bracketing options; see page 131 for Exposure Bracketing and page 69 for White Balance Bracketing.

Exposure Modes

The ∝200 provides a wide range of exposure modes—often called "operating" modes, a more logical term—selected by rotating the Mode dial (on the camera's left shoulder) to the appropriate icon or abbreviation. Let's take a look at each of the options, how they work, and when they might be useful.

Auto Mode [AUTO]

This was designed for maximum operating simplicity with the camera in total control of the aperture/shutter speed combination. In AUTO exposure, the camera uses its default settings, although you can set some overrides. Frankly, for anyone who wants to use a point-and-shoot approach, I suggest leaving all features at their factory-set default levels.

Program (P)

In this fully automatic mode the camera sets the shutter speed and aperture, but allows you to change the aperture/shutter speed combination. Initially, the camera sets an aperture (f/stop) and shutter speed to provide a correct exposure. You can temporarily change the combination of settings—called Program Shift—by rotating the camera's Control dial [icon] (in front of the shutter button).

The Program shift feature does not change the exposure (image brightness). It allows you to select from its various shutter speed/aperture combinations that maintain an equivalent exposure. (This concept—as well as many other aspects of exposure—is discussed later in this chapter.) When using flash in P mode, the Program shift feature is disengaged. All overrides can be used; once set, they remain set and the camera will not revert to its default settings.

Although P mode allows you to shift the aperture/shutter speed combination, it will revert to its own preferred aperture/shutter speed whenever the camera's light meter turns off. That's why I recommend using Aperture Priority (A) or Shutter Priority (S), discussed in the next sections. When you select an aperture (f/stop) in A mode or a shutter speed in S mode, the camera retains that setting and will not discard it as it would in Program mode. So if you have set f/22 or 1/15 second for instance, the camera will maintain those settings until you intentionally make a change.

Exposure Range Warnings

In the P, A, and S modes, it is possible to select an aperture and/or shutter speed that will produce incorrect exposure. That can occur when you set a very small aperture (such as f/22) or a very fast shutter speed (such as 1/1000 sec.) in low light, especially when using a low ISO level. It can also occur in very bright conditions when you set a very wide aperture (such as f/4), especially while using a very high ISO level. Fortunately, the camera provides an advance warning when your settings are likely to produce an exposure error (an excessively dark or bright image). The aperture and/or shutter speed numeral blinks in the viewfinder data panel. When that occurs, change the aperture or the shutter speed or the ISO level until the blinking stops.

Aperture Priority (A)

Selected by choosing the A on the Mode dial, this semi-automatic exposure mode allows you to set any aperture available on the lens using the Control dial. The camera then automatically sets a shutter speed that should yield a good exposure, according to its light meter's calculations. In some cases, exposure compensation will be required for an optimal exposure. All of the ∝200's functions are available and the camera will never override any of your settings.

Flash will always fire when it's popped up or when an accessory flash unit is on, even in bright scenes. When using flash, the camera will set a shutter speed no faster than the highest synchronization speed: 1/160 second. Aperture Priority mode is the best choice when you want to control depth of field.

Depth of Field: A Short Course

While the elements in your photos are usually three-dimensional, they are recorded on the sensor in two dimensions with a single plane of sharp focus. In other words, if you focus on a subject that is 3 meters (120 inches) from the camera, everything at the same distance will be sharply focused. Everything at different distances will appear less sharp.

114

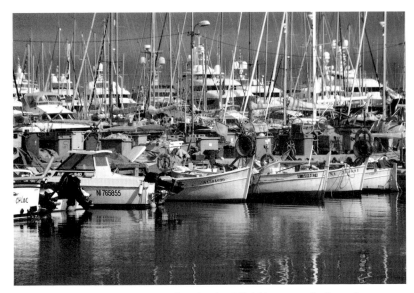

Except in action photography, depth of field is generally the primary concern, making Aperture Priority mode particularly useful. For this photo, taken with a moderate telephoto lens, f/11 was used for adequate depth of field to sharply render all of the boats.

However, when an image is viewed, there is an area in front of and behind the plane of sharp focus that is perceived to be in focus. This range of apparent sharpness is referred to as the depth of field. The factors that influence the amount of depth of field are:

• The focused distance
• The focal length in use
• The shooting aperture

If the focal length and subject distance are constant, depth of field will be shallower with large apertures (lower f/numbers) and more extensive with small apertures (higher f/numbers). If the aperture and focused distance are constant, depth of field will be shallower with longer lenses (telephoto range) and more extensive with shorter lenses

115

(wide-angle range). If the focal length and aperture are constant, depth of field will be greater at longer focused distances and shallower with closer focused distances.

These aspects should be considered when planning your composition and the look of the finished photograph. Aperture Priority (A) mode is particularly useful because it allows you to select a desired aperture that will be maintained until you change it. The camera sets an appropriate shutter speed for a "good" exposure, although you can use overrides for a brighter or darker effect.

Note: Today's lenses, including those compatible with the ∝200, use open-aperture metering. This means that they don't close down to the shooting aperture until a split second before the shutter opens to record an image. Until then, the aperture stays wide open, allowing the viewfinder to be as bright as possible for composing and focusing. That is useful but causes one problem: viewing a scene through the lens' maximum aperture doesn't allow you to judge depth of field at the shooting aperture. (Remember, as you set smaller apertures, such as f/16 vs. f/4, depth of field increases.)

The high-end Sony Alpha digital SLR cameras include a feature that closes the lens to the selected aperture so you can preview the depth of field as it will appear in the finished photograph. This feature is not available with the ∝200, which is considered to be an entry-level camera. Hence, you cannot preview the actual depth of field at any aperture. This is not generally a huge problem as long as you remember that wide apertures (such as f/4 or f/5.6) provide shallow depth of field and small apertures (such as f/16) provide more extensive depth of field. When getting the exact effect is important, take the same shot using several different apertures; one of the images should be just right.

Depth of Field Shooting Tips: In close-up photography, depth of field is limited. So to maximize it, choose a small aperture such as f/16. You may also wish to control the point of focus to further maximize depth of field. (Remember that focused distance is part of the formula that is especially important at close ranges.) If depth of field is not adequate, you can use a smaller aperture, or readjust the point of focus. For example, when photographing a flower, you may find that overall sharpness will be improved by focusing on a different part of the flower.

A soft, out-of-focus background is preferred for portrait photography because it will not draw the viewer's eye away from the subject. To accomplish this, choose a large aperture (small f/number, such as f/4 or f/5.6). Because telephoto lenses have less inherent depth of field than shorter focal lengths, they are ideal for isolating the subject against a softly blurred background.

For landscape photography, maximizing depth of field will render more of the scene in focus. Besides using a small aperture (larger f/number), controlling the point of focus will make the most of the depth of field. As a rule of thumb, depth of field will extend about 1/3 in front of the point of focus and 2/3 behind it. Thus, focusing somewhere in the front-to-middle portion of the scene will yield the greatest amount of sharpness. Take advantage of the lens or focal length to create a pleasing scenic view. Not only does a wide-angle lens allow you to capture sweeping vistas, but it also maximizes the depth of field in the photograph.

Shutter Priority (S)
When you want to control how motion is rendered in a photo, switch to the camera's S mode. This semi-automatic mode allows you to select a shutter speed, and the camera will set the appropriate f/stop for a suitable exposure. In some cases, exposure compensation will be required for a perfect exposure. Also remember the Exposure Range Warning; if you set a totally inappropriate shutter speed, a serious exposure error can occur.

When using flash in S mode, the camera will allow you to select a shutter speed as long as 30 seconds. However, when using flash, if you set a shutter speed faster than 1/160 second, the camera will override and revert to the maximum flash sync speed. All camera functions and overrides are available and your settings will remain active until you change them. Also, flash will always fire when it's popped up or when an accessory flash unit is on, even in bright scenes.

The following chart may be useful as a tool for learning the meaning of many common shutter speed abbreviations that you are likely to encounter in any camera exposure mode. It does not include every available option, but once you understand the concept, you'll have no difficulty in determining the exact shutter speed.

1000:	1/1000 second
60:	1/60 second
15:	1/15 second
1":	one second
1"5:	one and a half seconds
15":	fifteen seconds

Shutter Speed Considerations: Aside from using a shutter speed that will produce a sharp photo—without blur from camera shake—there's another important reason for selecting a slow or fast shutter speed: the ability to control how motion is portrayed in the photo. To appreciate the concept, take several shots of moving cars at a fast shutter speed such as 1/500 second on a bright sunny day. Do the same at a slow shutter speed such as 1/15 second. Analyze the resulting images and you should find that the first set is quite sharp while the second depicts the subject with motion blur.

This is useful for creative purposes, allowing you to control the way that a moving subject will appear in your images. Think of a waterfall for example. If you shoot at 1/500 second, the droplets of water will appear to be frozen in mid-air; that may not provide the flowing effect that you want. Put the camera on a tripod and switch to a shutter speed of 1/4 second and the water will be blurred, producing a convincing portrayal of the motion of flowing water.

When you select a very fast shutter speed in S mode, the camera will set a wider aperture to assure correct exposure, so depth of field will therefore be reduced. When using very fast shutter speeds, you may need to set a high ISO level, such as 400 on a sunny day or 800 on an overcast day.

When you select long shutter speeds, the camera will set a small aperture, so the image will exhibit greater depth of field. When using very long shutter speeds, you'll need to set a very low ISO level such as 100. (See the Exposure Range Warning on page 114 about exposure errors that can occur when you set an unusually long or slow shutter speed.)

In action photography, we often use fast shutter speeds to render the subject without motion blur. But sometimes it may be preferable to convey the feeling of motion by using a relatively slow shutter speed, such as 1/30 second. In this case the subject will be blurred instead of "frozen" or static.

This option works best with subjects moving across the frame from the left or right, thus traveling across your line of vision. Pan (move the camera) at the same speed your subject is moving. It helps to use a tripod with a pan head and to begin a little before tripping the shutter release. In the resulting image, the subject should be quite sharp, though with some motion blur, while the background will exhibit obvious blur. If the action is occurring close to the camera, try also using flash in Rear curtain sync mode (an option available with the **Fn** button) during a long exposure for some of your shots, as discussed in the chapter on flash photography (see page 164).

The pan/blur technique takes practice because it requires you to move the camera at exactly the right speed. You may need to shoot quite a few frames to get one that's nearly perfect, technically and aesthetically. Through persistent trial and error, you'll become more skilful with effective panning.

Manual (M)

Manual mode allows you to select any aperture/shutter speed combination, even if that will produce exposures that are entirely different than the camera recommended exposures. That's because Manual mode was intended to provide the ability to intentionally overexpose or underexpose an image for creative purposes. A scale in the viewfinder data panel, and in the LCD monitor, shows the amount of deviation from the meter-recommended exposure at the aperture and shutter speed you have set.

Experiment with M mode by selecting a shutter speed with the Control dial. In order to change the aperture, press and hold the exposure compensation button ⊡ on the back of the camera while rotating the Control dial. (This selection process can be reversed, using the [Ctrl dial setup] item in [Custom Menu 1 ✿1]; see page 89.)

Depending on your aperture/shutter speed selections, an image may be correctly exposed, according to the light meter (0 on the scale), or overexposed (+) or underexposed (-). The scale also shows the extent that your exposure will vary from the recommended "correct" exposure. A reading of +1 for example, indicates that the image will be overexposed by one Exposure Value (EV), while -1 indicates underexposure by one EV. The scale is marked in increments of one-third (0.33) EV.

One EV is equivalent to one aperture stop or one shutter-speed step. It's quite a large increment in digital photography; over or underexposure by one EV is generally obvious in an image. An EV factor of 0.33 is less noticeable in an image.

Manual exposure technique allows for controlling depth of field, shutter speed, and exposure simultaneously, but it is somewhat complex. Serious exposure errors can occur unless this mode is used with some expertise. Unless you are already proficient in Manual exposure control, you may want to experiment before relying on M mode for any serious photography.

Note: The ∝200 includes a feature called Manual Shift that allows you to change the aperture/shutter speed combination without affecting the exposure. To use this, set the aperture and shutter speed. Next, lock in that exposure level by pressing and holding the AEL button. Any subsequent changes—to f/stop for depth-of-field control, or shutter speed for control of the rendition of motion—will not change the image brightness. If you do enjoy shooting in fully manual mode, this feature may be helpful to you.

Bulb Exposure (BULB)

The longest shutter speed that you can select is 30 seconds, but there is another option for making even longer exposures: BULB. The term relates to a historically early photo accessory that used a blower bulb attached to a hose to trip the camera's shutter.

Set the Mode dial to M, and then decrease the shutter speed until the LCD display says [BULB]. Select a desired aperture by pressing and holding the [±] button while rotating the Control dial.

The camera's shutter will remain open as long as the shutter button is held all the way down. (An optional remote-control cable accessory should be used to trip and lock the shutter to eliminate camera shake.) A tripod must be used for sharp images during long exposures, and it is best to put the eyepiece cap in place to prevent light from entering through the viewfinder and affecting the exposure.

The camera's light meter is disengaged when BULB is selected, so you will need to use a handheld meter to calculate exposure. The Super SteadyShot system is also disabled. This option is most useful for night photography to record the moon and stars, a dark cityscape, or fireworks, for example. Many published articles in magazines and online provide hints on the exposure time and aperture that should provide a good exposure in those types of photography.

Scene Selection Modes

The ∝200 provides six different automatic Scene modes, or programs, that use "intelligent" automation to make suitable exposure settings for common situations and subjects. After selecting one of these scene-specific modes by choosing its icon on the Mode dial, you can set certain camera functions and overrides, such as ISO, drive mode, etc. Again, because these Scene Selection modes are intended for point-and-shoot picture taking, you'll probably want to use the camera's default settings.

Note: When any of the six Scene programs is selected, the camera automatically sets color saturation, contrast, and sharpening to a level that its computer deems to be appropriate for the subject type. Therefore, the Creative Style option and their overrides (discussed on pages 70-72) are not available for selection. Autofocus is also used, even if the camera is set to Manual focus mode. The Standard or Advanced D-Range Optimizer mode is activated automatically; the setting depends on the Scene mode that you are using.

Portrait 🙎 : Selects a moderately wide aperture to blur the background; a telephoto lens is recommended for an even more blurred or less distinct background. This mode is also said to "reproduce skin tones softly." Single-shot AF, AF-A autofocus, Wide Area AF, and Single-frame drive mode are automatically activated. The built-in flash will pop up automatically and fire in situations where it's needed.

Landscape ⛰ : Sets a moderately small aperture to optimize depth of field (zone of acceptably sharp focus, discussed on page 114) and uses the same AF and drive modes as Portrait. Color saturation is boosted for a rich effect. A landscape is usually too far from the camera for flash to be useful so the flash will not pop up or fire automatically in this mode.

Macro 🌷 : The term macro refers to close focusing, or filling the frame with a small subject. This program sets moderate apertures (such as f/5.6 or f/6.3) for moderate depth of field. That should render the subject sharply while blurring the background. The same AF and drive modes are used as in Portrait program. The built-in flash will pop up automatically and fire in situations where it's needed.

Note: Flash should not be used when a subject is less than a meter (40 inches) from the camera because the lens may block some of the light. If the subject is closer, switch to another mode that will not automatically use flash, such as P or the Flash Off mode. You can use accessory on-camera flash, but wireless off-camera flash is preferable for reasons discussed in the Flash chapter.

Sports action 🏃 : Favors fast shutter speeds to "freeze" a moving subject. Continuous AF and Continuous Advance drive mode are activated automatically. In low light however, you may need to set a higher ISO, such as 800 or 1600, for adequately fast shutter speeds to "freeze" the motion. (Do so with the ISO button as discussed on page 127.) Because an action subject is usually too far from the camera for flash to be useful, the flash will not pop up or fire automatically in this mode.

Sunset 🌄 : Very similar to Landscape program, but color rendition is optimized for richer reds, providing for a very "warm" effect.

Caution: Avoid viewing the sun directly or through the lens because doing so can damage your eyes.

Night Portrait 👤 : This mode is intended for using flash to take photos of a nearby subject against a moderately dark background, such as a person posing in front of a city scene at night. The camera sets a long shutter speed, as long as two seconds in dark locations. The flash fires at the start of the exposure to illuminate the nearby subject. During the long exposure time, the dark background has time to register on the camera's sensor, so that should be quite bright as well. Use a tripod to prevent blur from camera shake and ask your subject to stay perfectly still to prevent motion blur.

Flash Off ⚡ : While this is not a Scene mode per se, it is fully automatic. When selected, flash will not pop up or fire automatically. This mode is intended for taking snapshots at night, or in very dark locations without flash, so it's also called Night View program. It works well for scenes such as a city street with neon lights. The camera sets a very long shutter speed in low light, as long as eight seconds in very dark locations, making a tripod necessary for sharp photos without blur from camera shake. Moving subjects, such as vehicles, will be blurred due to the long exposure time.

Exposure: A Quick Primer

The term exposure in digital photography is defined as the amount of light that is required to create a likeness of the subject on the camera's CCD sensor. Ideally, the exposure should be "correct." This means the image should depict the scene with pure whites, rich, dark blacks, and mid-tones that are not excessively light or dark. Important detail should be visible in both highlight and shadow areas.

Every camera's light metering (measuring) system is calibrated to provide ideal exposure with average or mid-tone subjects such as grass, rocks, trees, or a gray card. When you use a conventional system, exposure errors are likely when the subject is very light in tone, such as a scene with bright snow, sand, sky, or water. In that case, the image may be too dark or underexposed. Conversely, a subject that is very dark in tone, such as a black lava field, may cause the photo to be too bright or overexposed.

At a given ISO setting, two factors control the amount of light that produces the image: the length of time that the camera's shutter is open and the size of the aperture (opening) in the lens. The selection of shutter speed and aperture can be left entirely to the camera or can be managed by the photographer using the camera's various exposure modes.

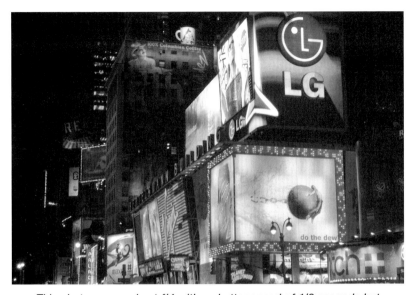

This photo was made at f/4 with a shutter speed of 1/8 seconds but many other aperture/shutter speed combinations would have produced exactly the same image brightness. It's important to fully appreciate the concept of "equivalent exposure" in order to understand how the automatic and semi-automatic exposure modes work.

The Role of Shutter Speed and Aperture

In order to create an image with the desired amount of light, the correct combination of shutter speed and aperture must be selected. This ensures that the image is not excessively bright or excessively dark. The longer the shutter speed, the greater the amount of light that will strike the image sensor. The larger the aperture selected, the more light that will enter during any given exposure time.

Shutter speeds are denoted in seconds, or fractions of a second. Aperture size is denoted with f/numbers, also called f/stops. The smaller the f/number, the larger the aperture size. A wide aperture such as f/4 will allow far more light to enter the camera than a small aperture such as f/16 during any given time period. The camera's auto exposure system considers scene brightness and sets an f/stop and shutter speed that should produce a well-exposed image.

Note: Even the most sophisticated light meter—such as the honeycomb pattern system—will not always produce a perfect exposure. Extremely light or dark-toned subjects may cause exposure errors. Also, an accurate exposure may not be the most pleasing or most appropriate for creative expression. That's why the ∝200 includes options for adjusting the exposure.

Equivalent Exposure

The camera's shutter speed and aperture steps (or stops) both increase and decrease exposure in equal amounts. Each full step increment doubles or halves the amount of light reaching the sensor. Thus, if you decrease the length of the shutter speed by one full stop and increase the size of the aperture by one full stop, the exposure will remain the same. Once the meter has determined the exposure for a scene, you can change the aperture or shutter speed in use, as long as you make a corresponding change in the other.

Practically, this allows you to fine tune the appearance of the image without changing exposure. In Aperture Priority mode, you can change the aperture (f/stop) to modify the depth of field in a photo. When you do so, the camera will change the shutter speed to maintain the same—or equivalent—exposure. In Shutter Priority mode you can change the shutter speed to influence the rendition of motion. If you do so, the camera will change the aperture (f/stop) to maintain the same (equivalent) exposure.

Measuring Brightness

There once was a time when cameras did not contain any built-in system for measuring subject brightness. In those days you needed to use an accessory light meter or rely on estimates, experience, or expertise to make appropriate settings.

The ∝200 includes three light metering options. These are the 40-segment honeycomb pattern Multi Segment system that uses artificial intelligence, the old-style Center Weighted system, and Spot metering. You'll find specifics about each later in this chapter.

ISO (Sensitivity)

The amount of light required for an accurate exposure depends on the ISO setting you have selected on the camera. ISO is an international standard that was developed for quantifying a film's sensitivity to light. While digital cameras don't use film, ISO numbers are still used to define the camera's sensitivity, or gain (amplification). A low ISO number such as 100 denotes low sensitivity to light. A high ISO number such as 800 or 1600 denotes high sensitivity to light. After you set an ISO level, this data is automatically taken into account by the camera's light meter when making calculations about the aperture and shutter speed combination that should produce a good exposure.

Note: ISO numbers are mathematically proportional, as are shutter speeds and f/stops. As you double or halve the ISO number, you double or halve the sensitivity. For instance, at ISO 800, half as much light is required for a good exposure as at ISO 400. Conversely, at ISO 1600, twice as much light is required for a good exposure as at ISO 3200.

The ∝200 allows you to choose an ISO from 100 to 3200, although you'll rarely need to use the highest option. Since digital noise (graininess) increases with ISO, select ISO 100 for the best image quality, and higher ISO levels as needed for faster shutter speeds.

Select an ISO level by pressing the ISO button and scrolling to the desired option with the Controller keys. Press the central button to confirm your selection.

One of the ISO choices is AUTO (not to be confused with AUTO exposure mode). When it is selected, the camera will set a low ISO in bright light and a higher ISO in darker conditions to minimize the risk of blur from camera shake. (The Super SteadyShot function is useful for this purpose too, but it cannot compensate for subject movement or for camera shake at extremely long shutter speeds.)

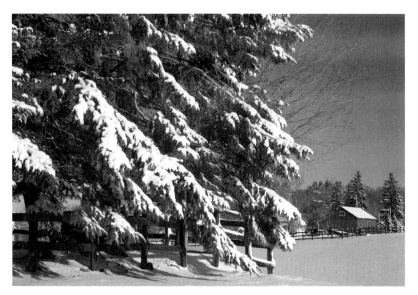

Multi-segment metering is a fine choice for a wide range of subjects, but it cannot always provide perfect exposures, particularly when a scene includes a large expanse of snow, water, sand, or other light-toned subjects. In this situation, for example, Spot metering from a mid-tone area (the barn) provided the best overall exposure.

Metering Method

It's important to understand the camera's light metering strategies in each of the three options available. To find these, press the **Fn** button, scroll to the [Metering mode] item and press the central button. You can now scroll to the one you want; then press the central button to confirm your selection. The following options are available:

Multi Segment Metering

This system employs a 40-segment honeycomb pattern and artificial intelligence to evaluate brightness in all areas of a scene. The on-board computer also considers subject distance if you are using a Maxxum/Dynax D series lens (with distance data detector chip) or any Sony or Carl Zeiss ZA lens. When the camera is set to autofocus, subject position data provided by the AF system is also considered in the metering computer's analysis.

Because the system compares exposure data with pre-programmed exposure models, it is quite successful at metering subjects with unusual reflectance. For example, in strong backlighting—a friend posing against a setting sun, for example—the system increases exposure automatically to reduce the risk of a dark image. It uses the same strategy for any scene with high reflectance, whether a sunny, snow-covered landscape, or a close-up of a bride in white. The metering system should also compensate for a dark-toned subject, such as a lava field, reducing exposure to render it as black, instead of gray.

While this is a sophisticated metering system that often provides close to optimal exposures, its recommendations may not always be ideal. Scenes that are difficult to meter may sometimes require slight adjustments using exposure compensation or bracketing, discussed later in this chapter.

Slight exposure errors may or may not be a problem, depending on whether or not you can correct the errors with image processing software. But even when shooting with RAW, which offers more capacity than JPEG for post-shooting exposure correction without degrading image quality, it is worth taking the time to get a well-exposed image in-camera, using exposure compensation if necessary.

Spot Metering

Spot metering measures only the portion of the scene within the small circular area in the center of the viewfinder. To use it, point the lens so that the central circle etched on the viewing screen covers the target you intend to meter.

One of the most valuable uses of Spot metering is to measure light values in different parts of a scene for comparison or to determine the exposure gradient in the scene. Another common scenario is a spot lit performer (small in the frame) against a dark background. Or you might want to take the light meter reading from a small mid-tone subject located in very bright surroundings, such as a cabin in a snowy landscape. These types of scenes often produce less than optimal exposures with other metering patterns.

In the above cases, spot meter your primary subject, then press and hold the AEL (Autoexposure Lock) button to make sure that the locked-in exposure does not change while you recompose. When you take the shot, the exposure will be optimized for the primary subject. (See the lengthy discussion of various exposure issues, including Autoexposure Lock, later in this chapter.)

With experience, this is a useful type of metering. But it can also be tricky because the exposure is significantly affected by the brightness of the selected area. If the target is a mid-tone (a tanned face, for example), the exposure will be accurate. But if you take a spot meter reading of a light-toned area (such as a snowman), underexposure will occur. And if you spot meter a dark area (such as a black cat), the image will be overexposed. Consequently, spot metering is intended primarily for experienced photographers with some expertise in judging tonal values and knowing when exposure compensation must be applied.

Center Weighted Metering
This option measures brightness over most of the scene and averages the data, but it applies extra weight to a large central area. The system does not employ any "intelligent" evaluation, so it's more likely to produce exposure errors than the Multi Segment meter.

Photographers who have worked extensively with older film cameras using Center Weighted metering may want to use this option with the ∝200 as well. It will often require the use of exposure compensation, with the appropriate amount based on experience or rules of thumb. When applied with expertise, this technique can produce excellent exposures. However, in general you will get better results with the camera's Multi Segment metering system. You are also better off using Spot rather than Center Weighted metering when it is advantageous to precisely meter a small area of a scene.

Exposure Compensation

After taking a photo in the camera's P, A, or S mode, check it on the LCD monitor. If you think it's too bright or too dark, set some exposure compensation and re-shoot. Access exposure compensation with the 🔲 button (on back of camera, right of viewfinder). While pressing and holding that button, rotate the Control dial 🔛 to the right to select a plus (+) value for a brighter image, or to the right for a minus (–) value for a darker image. Watch the scale in the LCD monitor change to reflect your settings and stop when you reach a desired level of compensation.

The ∝200 allows you to make changes toward the plus side or the minus side in 1/3 (0.33) EV increments. EV denotes exposure value, and one full EV change equals one full aperture stop or one full shutter speed step, either of which doubles or halves the light.

When shooting with Multi Segment metering, few scenes will require more than a +1 or –2/3 (or -0.7) EV of exposure compensation. Take a shot without compensation and review it in the Playback mode, preferably using the histogram (discussed on page 136) for an exposure analysis. If the photo is too dark, set some (+) compensation and take the shot again. If the photo is too bright, set some (–) compensation before re-shooting.

Exposure Bracketing

This function allows you to shoot three successive frames while the camera automatically shifts the exposure for each photo. This increases your chances of getting the optimal exposure in one photo with any given subject in any given lighting condition. Exposure bracketing is selected with the drive button ⟳/⧉ on top of the camera and scrolling with the Controller keys to the desired choice. Then, press the central button to confirm your selection.

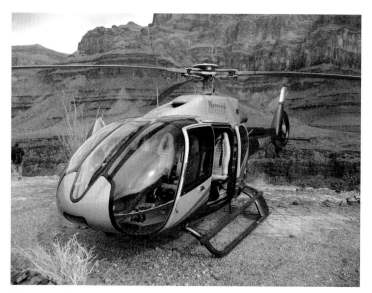

A scene of this type, consisiting mostly of mid-tones, should provide a very good exposure with either Multi-segment or Center Weighted metering. Use exposure compensation and/or bracketing only in situations where a scene consists primarily of light or dark toned areas that are likely to cause the light meter to provide incorrect exposures.

Note: Bracketing cannot be selected when the camera is set to the AUTO mode or any of the Scene modes such as Landscape, Portrait, etc. It will work in other modes, including Manual (M) mode. While first experimenting, try Bracketing with the mode dial set to P for Program mode. When you no longer wish to bracket exposures, be sure to switch to one of the other drive modes with the ☉/ 🖳 button.

Use any of the following options to take three photos. The first will be exposed as per the light meter's recommendation (the "base" exposure). The second photo will be darker (with some automatically applied (–) compensation) while the third will be brighter (with some automatically applied (+) compensation). One of the three frames should be acceptable or very good in terms of exposure.

- **BRK C * 0.3 EV**: Pressing and holding the shutter button causes the camera to fire three frames in a continuous burst with a slight 0.3 EV (or 1/3 EV) difference in exposure.

- **BRK C * 0.7 EV**: This choice also fires three frames in a continuous burst but with a greater difference in each exposure: 0.7 EV (or 2/3 EV).

Note: In continuous bracketing, only the last image of the series will be displayed in the LCD monitor. If you want to review all three, use the camera's Playback ▶ mode.

- **BRK S * 0.3 EV**: Uses Single frame advance; press the shutter button separately three consecutive times to take three photos, each with a 0.3 EV difference in exposure.

- **BRK S * 0.7 EV**: This works in the same manner but applies a greater exposure adjustment difference of 0.7 EV.

Bracketing can be useful when you are not certain how much exposure compensation to set, or whether or not some plus or minus compensation would produce the most visually pleasing exposure. When using bracketing, you can first apply general exposure compensation such as +2/3 EV (0.77 EV) before taking close-up photos of a white egret, for example.

Autoexposure Lock (AEL)

As mentioned in previous sections of this chapter, the ∝200 allows you to take a light meter reading from a desired area and lock in the exposure value. That can be useful for basing the exposure on a mid-tone area such as the palm trees instead of bright sand at a beach. When the camera is set for Multi Segment metering and for Autofocus, Autoexposure Lock is provided by the shutter release button. As long as you maintain slight pressure, the exposure remains locked; this allows you to take a light meter reading from a desired area and then recompose without losing the original exposure value.

When using Center Weighted or Spot metering however—
or when using manual focus—you must press the AEL button
to record an exposure value, and keep it depressed while
recomposing. This feature is particularly useful when spot
metering a small, off-center subject as discussed in the Spot
metering section. While AE Lock is active a ✱ symbol
appears in the viewfinder data panel. (The [AEL button] item
in [Custom Menu 1 ✿ 1] allows you to modify the button's
operation to a toggle switch as discussed on page 88.)

Experiment with AE Lock using Spot metering. Point the
lens at the area you wish to meter and press the AEL button
on the back of the camera; this locks in the exposure value.
Keep the button depressed as you recompose to ensure that
the exposure does not change. When you're ready to take
the shot, depress the shutter release button; the camera will
expose the image for the area that you metered.

If you plan to use the AEL technique, set some exposure
compensation if your target is light-toned or dark-toned. This
should help to assure correct exposure. For example, try setting +1.3 if you plan to take the Spot meter reading from a
performer's white costume. Or set -2/3 or -1 if taking the
meter reading from a black cat. Then activate the AEL,
recompose for the desired framing, and take the shot. (If
metering a mid-tone subject, such as foliage or a tanned
face, no exposure compensation should be necessary.)

Note: Do not use the AEL button when flash is active since
that will produce an underexposed, very dark image. The
AEL button is not intended for use in flash photography.
However, when using Multi Segment metering, the ∝200
does provide Autoexposure lock with slight pressure on the
shutter release button.

Exposure Evaluation

In addition to visual evaluation of images on the LCD monitor, there are two other methods for analyzing exposure: the histogram and the Luminance limit warning. Both are available in instant playback and in the camera's full Playback mode ▶ by pressing the DISP button. In Playback mode you may need to press the DISP button more than once to reach the screen with the histograms.

Although the actual image is smaller, you will find four scales—graphs called histograms—on the right side of the monitor indicating the brightness distribution in the image. Also, any excessively bright or dark areas will blink within the displayed image, thanks to the Luminance limit warning

Luminance Limit Warning

This feature highlights areas of a photo that exhibit some loss of detail. When bright areas of the displayed image flash, highlights are "blown out," or too bright to hold detail. When shadow areas flash, they are "blocked up," or too dark to show detail.

Each type of warning (highlight or shadow) flashes alternately; the display uses a different type of pattern for each in order to avoid confusion. This Luminance limit warning is not as informative as the histogram display, but it's logical, intuitive, and easier to interpret. It can certainly help you avoid the most serious exposure problems.

Consider a situation where highlight detail or texture is important, as in a bride's dress or the texture of a flower petal. After taking a shot, check the image, looking closely for a highlight warning in the pertinent area. If it flashes, you'll probably want to re-shoot. Set a –0.3 exposure compensation; review the image in Playback mode ▶ and check for a warning. If necessary, re-shoot again, using a –0.7 exposure compensation factor, and check the image for a highlight warning. Keep an eye on shadow warnings at the same time if there is also important detail in shadow areas.

Hint: Although highlight detail is often the most important, be careful to avoid underexposure that will need to
be corrected with imaging software. When you underexpose and subsequently lighten the images in a computer,
digital noise will be very obvious; in images made at ISO
800 and above, the graininess can be objectionable. When
possible, re-shoot several times, using different levels of
exposure compensation for each shot. You can always
darken the image in the computer, which will not affect
digital noise. However, lightening the shadow areas in
post processing will usually cause any preexisting noise to
be more noticeable.

Sometimes shadow detail or texture is important—as in
the fur of your black cat. In that case, pay attention to the
shadow warning. If an important shadow area blinks, you
may well choose to re-shoot. Set a bit of plus compensation
to increase the exposure, allowing the camera to record
more detail. But beware of overexposing important highlights; setting too much plus exposure compensation can
produce flashing in the highlight areas.

The Histogram
The histogram is of a graph that appears on the LCD monitor
indicating brightness distribution from black (on the left side
of the graph) to white (on the right side) along the horizontal
axis. The ∝200 displays four of these graphs but the top one
—called the Luminance histogram—is the most valuable.
The others relate to individual color channels are much
more difficult to interpret. That's why I'll discuss only the
Luminance histogram.

Take a photo that consists primarily of dark areas (such as
a lava field) and the graph will be weighted to the left. Conversely, an image consisting primarily of light tones (such as
a snowy landscape) will be heavily weighted to the right.
Mid-tone brightness distribution is represented in the central
area of the graph. The vertical axis indicates the pixel quantity existing for the different levels of brightness.

If the graph rises as a typical bell-shaped curve, from the bottom left corner of the histogram to a peak in the middle, then descends to the bottom right corner, all the tones of the scene are captured. If the graph starts or ends too far up on either the left or right vertical axis of the histogram, so that the "slope" looks like it is cut off, then the camera is cutting off data from those areas. Some loss of detail is inevitable when the contrast range is beyond the capabilities of the camera—a black vehicle for instance, surrounded by extremely bright sky or sand, for example.

There is no single "ideal" histogram however. For instance, a photo of groomsmen in black tuxedos against a navy blue wall consists primarily of dark tones. Even if it is perfectly exposed, the histogram will be heavily weighted towards the dark (left) side of the graph. And a winter land-scape scene that's perfectly exposed will be weighted heavily toward the bright (right) side of the graph. The key in both cases is to avoid a loss of detail or texture in important areas of the scene.

To render detail in highlight areas, control exposure so the slope on the right reaches the bottom of the graph before it hits the right vertical axis and "drops off" that side. If a scene includes detail elements in shadow areas, manage exposure so that the left side of the slope reaches the bottom of the histogram before it hits the left vertical axis, realizing that the "real" world is not perfect and you can't always pro-duce a perfect exposure.

Check the histogram after taking a shot and, if necessary, re-shoot using a plus or minus exposure compensation set-ting. Then check the histogram again for the new image. Also see whether the compensation has produced any unde-sired blown highlights or blocked shadows. Of course, when shadow detail is most important, you may need to tolerate some loss of detail in the brightest areas, and vice versa.

Both the Luminance limit warning and the Luminance his-togram provide feedback on exposure and contrast. Once

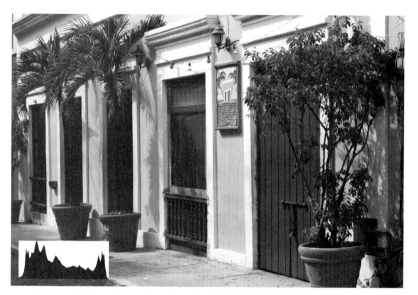

Image A. There's no single "perfect" histogram but the graph for this photo does indicate an exposure which is satisfactory, with detail in both highlight and shadow areas.

you review the information they provide, you can choose to re-shoot the image with a different exposure compensation level and/or a different contrast level. Although some people count on "fixing" exposure problems with imaging software, you can't add detail that was never captured in the first place. Whether shooting JPEGs or RAW files, always get the best image possible in camera.

Image A: If the graph rises from the bottom left corner of the histogram, then descends towards the bottom right corner, all the tones of the scene are captured. (There may be a few peaks and valleys involved, but the graph still rises from the left and ends very close to the right axis).The image will include pure black, pure white, and a good distribution of mid-tones, for an exposure that's correct overall.

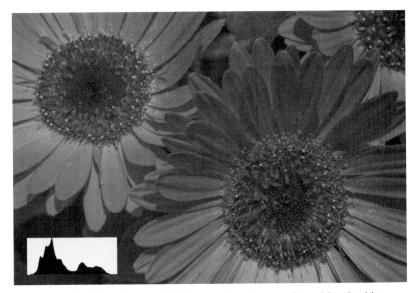

Image B. This photo exhbits low contrast as confirmed by the histogram and would require work in image editing software for a better exposure.

Image B: With some images, the slope will drop before it reaches either the left or right side of the scale. In other words, the graph starts too far in from one or both edges. This indicates that the image does not contain rich dark blacks or bright pure white tones. (Remember, black is represented on the left of the graph and white on the right.)

The image consists primarily of mid-tones and grayish blacks and grayish whites. This does not necessarily mean poor exposure; in fact, it signifies low contrast. That's easy to correct in the computer, or by setting a slightly higher contrast level in-camera (see page 74). Of course, you may decide to set some plus or minus exposure compensation before taking the shot again. That will produce brighter whites or darker black tones.

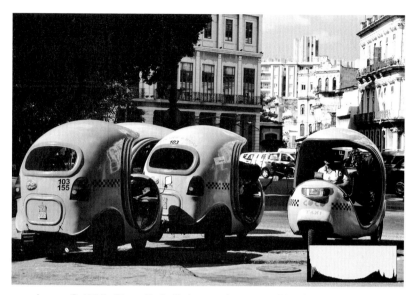

Image C. While it's unlikely that your photos would exhibit such ultra-high contrast, this image and its histogram confirm a loss of detail in both highlight and shadow areas.

Image C: With extremely high contrast subjects (including very dark shadow areas plus very bright highlights), the histogram may show a slope that is cut off at both ends. This indicates that detail will be lost in both highlight and shadow areas. Dark sections of your photo may fade to black, and brighter sections may appear completely washed out.

Try re-shooting an image of this type, using a low contrast setting in-camera. Also try using the Advanced D-Range Optimizer function as discussed in the next section. For nearby subjects, try using flash to even out the lighting for gentler overall contrast. If the light is changing, wait until a cloud covers the sun, moderating excessive contrast.

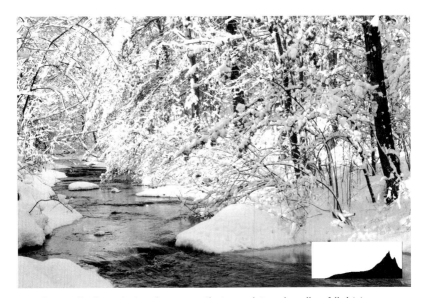

Image D. Any photo of a scene that consists primarily of light tones will produce a histogram that's heavily weighted to the right, but in this case, the graph also indicates overexposure: a loss of detail in important highlight areas.

Image D: In some images, such as a portrait of a bride in white or a sunlit flower, highlight details are important. In those cases, be sure the slope on the right reaches the bottom of the graph before it hits the right side. Otherwise, the image will not hold detail in bright areas of the photo; these details will be blown out as demonstrated in the whites of this lunch-time vendor. Re-shoot after setting a minus exposure compensation setting.

D-Range Optimizer

Although technically not considered an exposure control, D-Range Optimizer does affect exposure. (The term D-range refers to dynamic range or tonal values in a photo.) Different effects are provided by the Standard **D-R** mode and the Advanced **D-R+** mode. In a nutshell, Standard mode lightens shadow areas in underexposed images while Advanced mode, somewhat more sophisticated, lightens shadow areas and darkens highlight areas in scenes that you photograph under extremely harsh, contrasty light, attempting to retain detail in both dark areas and very bright areas. See pages 24-25 for a further explanation.

The Standard DR mode (used for this photo) provides a moderate *improvement in highlight and shadow detail, making this option suitable for frequent use. Switch to the Advanced DR mode only when necessary: for scenes with extreme contrast requiring more aggressive in-camera processing.*

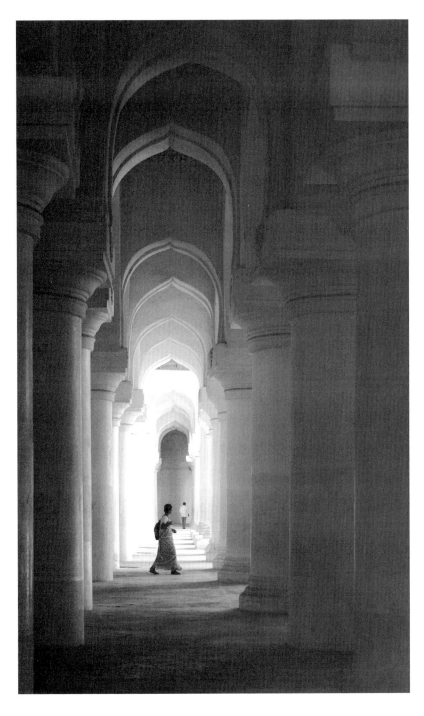

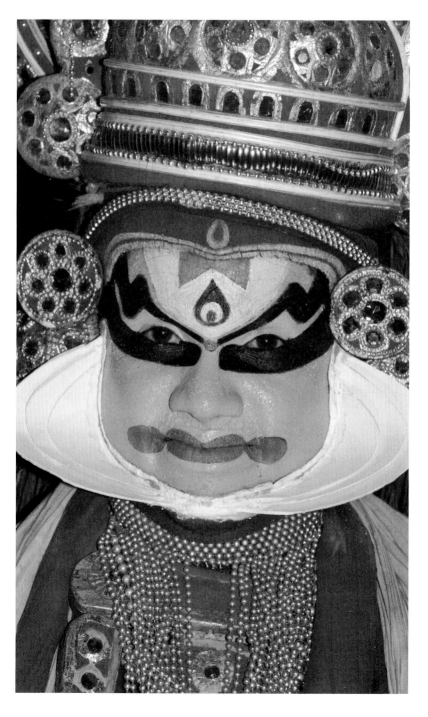

Flash Photography

Electronic flash is not just a supplement for insufficient lighting—it can also be a great tool for creative photography. Flash is highly controllable, its color is precise, and the results are repeatable. However, many photographers shy away from using on-camera flash because it can be harsh and unflattering, and taking the flash off the camera used to be a complicated procedure with less than sure results. The sophisticated flash options available with the ∝200—especially with a compatible accessory flash unit—eliminate many of these concerns. Remember too, the LCD monitor provides instantaneous feedback showing whether the flash exposure was right or not. You can make adjustments if you are not satisfied with your flash exposure and take the photo again.

However, it is still helpful to understand the basics of how flash photography works. The following are some of the important standards.

Flash photography can be simple and quick, but more advanced lighting effects are also possible with accessories and other exposure modes. Because time was tight when making this photo, direct on-camera flash and P mode were used. Given more time to adjust various settings, much better results would have been possible with some of the alterntatives discussed in this chapter.

Flash Basics

The Inverse Square Law

It's not difficult to understand one of the essential concepts at work with flash photography. As light travels away from its source it also spreads outward, losing intensity. Consequently the Inverse Square Law, a fundamental principle of light, says that light intensity is reduced by a factor of four as the distance from a source—in this case your flash unit—doubles. Light level drops dramatically according to distance. In fact, if you are 3 feet (0.9 m) from your subject, you need four times as much light to maintain the same level of exposure when you move 6 feet (1.8 m) away from the subject.

Guide Numbers

Guide numbers (GN) are a comparative reference used to quantify flash output. They are expressed in terms of ISO, in feet and/or meters. The formula to determine guide numbers is GN = distance x aperture. So—according to the Inverse Square Law—a flash unit with a GN of 100 in feet (30.5 m) puts out four times the amount of light as one with a GN of 50 in feet (15.25 m). If your accessory flash has a zoom head, the GN will vary according to the zoom setting.

Flash Synchronization

The ∝200 has a focal plane shutter that consists of two shutter curtains. When you press the shutter release button, the first curtain opens to uncover the camera's sensor and the second curtain covers it. The shutter speed determines the length of time between the first curtain opening and the second curtain closing. To take a photo with flash, the flash must fire when the camera's first shutter curtain is open across the entire frame and before the second curtain begins to close. The fastest speed at which the flash fires while the shutter is fully open is called the maximum flash synchronization speed or sync speed. In fact, in flash photography, we always refer to shutter speed as sync speed.

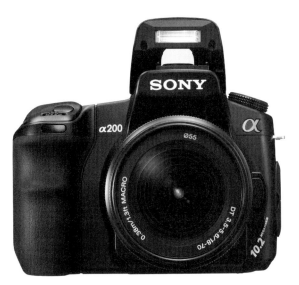

The built-in flash pops up when needed and fires automatically in some of the Scene modes. In other modes, it can be manually raised and will always fire when it's in the up position. While this built-in amenity is usually used for snapshots, all of the camera's flash functions are available, offering some versatility that makes built-in flash useful, especially for adding a bit of extra light to people pictures in outdoor photography.

The ∝200 has a maximum sync speed of 1/160 second. When using the built-in flash or a dedicated accessory flash, the camera will not let you set a shutter speed faster than that maximum sync speed. (Some accessory flash units have a high-speed sync feature that allows for using much faster shutter speeds. See page 169.) Naturally, you or the camera can set longer shutter (sync) speeds in flash photography.

The Built-In Flash

In order to operate the built-in flash when the camera's mode selector dial is set to P, A, S, or M, you must first manually raise it. Press the ⚡ button on the left side of the camera (above the AF/MF switch) and the built-in tube will pop up. It will then always fire, regardless of the lighting conditions. You can select any of the options available in the

Flash Modes item in the Function sub-menu (accessed by pressing the camera's **Fn** button): Fill-flash, Slow sync, Rear sync, and Wireless. (Each will be discussed in detail in this chapter.) You can also use flash exposure compensation (see page 160) to increase or decrease flash intensity.

When the camera's mode selector dial is set to AUTO or any of the Scene Selection modes—Landscape, Macro, Portrait, Sports Action, Night Portrait, or Sunset—you will not be able to manually pop the built-in flash up. Flash control is totally controlled by the camera, as discussed in the Exposure Modes section of Chapter 5. Flash will never pop up or fire in Landscape, Sports Action, or Sunset mode; in the other modes mentioned above it will pop up and fire when necessary.

Good photos are definitely possible in the AUTO, Portrait, Macro, and Night Portrait modes in low light, even though flash control is totally automatic. By the time you have composed and focused, the flash should be charged and ready to fire, confirmed by a ⚡ symbol in the viewfinder data panel. The camera will set a suitable aperture and shutter speed. It will also set a suitable flash power output, or intensity level. The image should be well exposed as long as your subject is within the flash range (see opposite page).

Regardless of the camera mode that you use, the flash must recycle or recharge after firing. You cannot take the next shot while the ⚡ symbol is blinking; that signal indicates that the flash unit is not yet ready to fire. When the blinking stops, you can take the next flash photo.

Note: Some of the flash features to be discussed in this chapter can be set when the ∝200 is used in its AUTO exposure mode and in certain Scene Selection modes, but that is not recommended because these modes are intended for snap shooting. Hence, all further discussions about flash options will refer to photography in the camera's P, A, S, or M exposure modes.

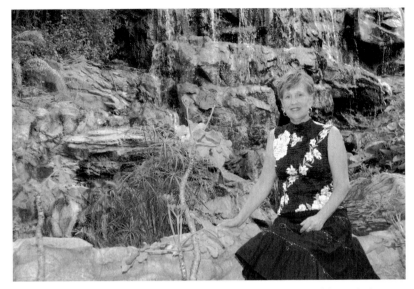

The effective range of the built-in flash depends on the ISO level, the aperture (f/stop) that's used, and the ambient lighting conditions. For this outdoor photo made in the evening at f/11 (a small aperture), with the subject only 2 meters (about 6 feet) from the camera, flash range was adequate, even at ISO 400.

Flash Range

The built-in unit is not particularly powerful, but it has adequate range for most snapshots and people pictures. The effective range varies with the aperture that's used: it's greater at larger apertures (f/4 for example) than at smaller ones (f/11). Effective range also varies depending on the ISO selected: it's greater at higher ISO settings. The following chart provides effective flash range at f/4, a common maximum aperture at the short end of many variable aperture zoom lenses, and at f/5.6, a maximum aperture that's common with these lenses at the medium to longer focal lengths.

ISO Setting	f/4	f/5.6
100	1 - 3m 3.3 - 9.8 ft.	1 - 2.1m 3.3 - 6.7 ft.
200	1 - 4.3m 3.3 - 14 ft.	1 - 3m 3.3 - 9.8 ft.
400	1- 6m 3.3 - 20 ft.	1 - 4.3m 3.3 - 14 ft.
800	1.4 - 8.6m 4.6 - 28 ft.	1 - 6m 3.3 - 20 ft.
1600	2 - 12m 6.6 - 39 ft.	1.4 - 8.6m 4.6 - 28 ft.
3200	2.8 - 17m 9.2 - 56 ft.	2 - 12m 6.6 - 39 ft.

Hint: Photocopy this chart and carry it in your camera bag along with the wallet card found in the back of this book. And don't ignore the minimum range. Moving very close for a frame-filling close-up—especially when using a high ISO setting—can produce excessively bright flash photos.

Although the flash range is impressive at ISO 800 and par-ticularly at ISO 3200, remember that image quality will be lower at very high ISO levels due to increased digital noise. Consequently, you might consider buying one of the power-ful accessory Sony HVL-AM series flash units (with at least double the range). This will allow you to shoot at lower ISO settings for superior image quality.

Accessory Flash Units

The ∝200 supports full-featured flash photography with the compatible accessory flash units. These include the Sony HVL-F56AM, HVL-F36AM, and the newer HVL-F42AM mod-els, as well as (discontinued) Maxxum/Dynax D and HS-D series flash units. With these you can take advantage of wireless off-camera TTL flash, high-sync speed flash, rear-

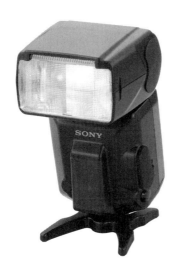

Sony now makes three accessory flash units, with the HVL-56AM offering the greatest power output and versatility.

curtain flash synchronization, bounce flash, and advanced off-camera setups for sophisticated flash effects discussed in this chapter.

The ∝200 is also compatible with the HVL-MT24AM Macro Twin Flash Kit intended specifically for macro photography: extremely close focusing, using a macro lens. While some older Maxxum/Dynax flash units—not bearing the HS-D or D series designation— can also be used with the ∝200, they require the optional Sony Flash Shoe Adapter FA-SA1AM, and they must also be used in Manual flash mode—a somewhat complicated and inconvenient process.

The fully compatible or dedicated flash units also allow you to utilize sophisticated ADI (Advanced Distance Integration) flash metering. However, that also requires the use of D-series Maxxum/Dynax lenses, Sony lenses, or the Carl Zeiss ZA series designed for the Alpha cameras. All of these lenses include the distance data detector chip. ADI flash uses distance information from the appropriate lenses to control the flash output and is less affected by very bright or very dark subjects than is Pre-flash TTL metering, which does not use distance information (see page 155). (The flash metering system cannot employ distance data when non D-series lenses are used.)

Sony Flash Units
At the time this guide was prepared, Sony marketed the following flash units.

HVL-F56AM: This is a large model with high power output. Its Guide Number (GN) is 185/56 (feet/meters) at ISO 100 using the 85mm zoom head setting. This model features an illuminated LCD data panel, power zoom flash head to match focal lengths from 24mm to 85mm, wide-angle diffusion panel (for use with lenses as short as 17mm), focus-assist illuminator, plus several functions for additional creative options. In addition to conventional upward tilt capability, this unit allows for tilting the head 10° downward for close-up photography, and can be rotated to the side for bouncing flash from a wall.

HVL-F42AM: This slightly smaller unit is less powerful, with a GN of 42/13 (feet/meters) at ISO 100 when the zoom head is at the 105mm setting. It includes nearly all of the features of the larger model, and offers greater versatility with 24mm to 105mm zoom head settings, but omits the downward tilt capability. Thanks to improved circuitry, this model can recycle (recharge) 38% more quickly than the less powerful HVL-F36AM model, discussed below.

Flash HVL-F36AM: This is a more compact unit with lower power. The GN is 118/36 (feet/meters) at ISO 100 using the 85mm zoom head setting. It lacks an LCD data panel, but has a power zoom flash head to match focal lengths from 24mm to 85mm, a wide-angle diffusion panel (for use with lenses as short as 17mm), and a focus-assist illuminator. The head only tilts upward for bouncing flash off a ceiling.

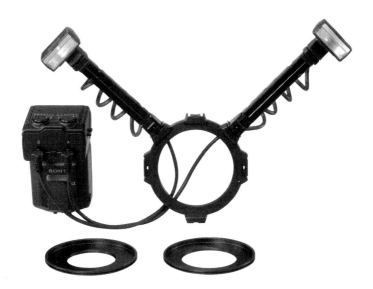

The Sony Macro Twin Flash Kit HVL-MT24AM.

Macro Flash Units

The Sony Macro Twin Flash Kit HVL-MT24AM is a large piece of equipment consisting of a controller unit that mounts in the camera's hot shoe and two distinct flash tubes on adjustable arms, mounted on a ring that attaches to the front of a macro lens. The two primary components are connected with a cable that's included in the kit. Either or both flash tubes can be used at any time and their position can be modified by rotating the attaching ring. Each flash head has a GN of 40/12 (feet/meters). The Twin Flash Kit comes with 49mm and 55mm adaptor rings, wide-angle diffusion panels, and a storage pouch.

Macro Ring Light HVL-RLAM: This is a professional caliber unit designed for extreme close-up photography with a Macro lens. It does not provide as many automatic features and must be used with the flash shoe adapter FA-SA1M; this is necessary for mounting the controller unit in the hot shoe of any of the Sony

Alpha camera or the discontinued Maxxum/Dynax 5D and 7D cameras. The Macro Ring Light is quite powerful with a GN of 79/24 (feet/meters) at ISO 100. Its circular head includes four flash tubes that can be individually illuminated. Use all four for even lighting, or select specific tubes for more directional lighting. The kit includes 49mm and 55mm adapter rings for attaching the ring light to the front of a macro lens.

Flash Metering Options

The camera allows you to select from two options for flash metering control in the Recording Menu **📷** 1 . The following information clarifies some of the concepts relating to those options.

ADI Flash (Advanced Distance Integration)
This is the most sophisticated TTL (through the lens) metering option. It's available only when using Sony, Carl Zeiss ZA, or Maxxum/Dynax D-series lenses and either the built-in flash or a fully compatible accessory flash unit. The camera's microcomputer uses focus distance data provided by the lens, plus aperture and ISO information, to set the flash exposure. This increases the odds of a good exposure because it is less influenced by high or low subject reflectance, therefore more likely to produce a good exposure with white or black subjects that might otherwise lead to under or overexposure, respectively. I recommend this option for those who use a compatible lens and the built-in flash or a fully dedicated external flash unit.

Note: If the AF system is unable to find focus, or if you're using manual focus, the camera will automatically switch to the other option: Pre-flash TTL control. The same will occur when using an accessory flash for wireless off-camera flash photography or a Maxxum/Dynax lens without the D-series designation. Finally, note that Sony recommends selecting the Pre-flash TTL mode when using filters that reduce light transmission (such as a polarizer) or when utilizing an accessory flash unit's wide-angle adapter (diffuser).

154

Pre-Flash

This is the standard TTL flash metering mode for use with non D-series lenses or in the circumstances noted above. With this technology, a brief burst of flash is fired before an exposure is made. The camera's microcomputer analyzes the scene based on the pre-flash to determine the appropriate light output for exposure. Most of your flash exposures will be fine, unless the subject is unusually light or dark, or is located against a very bright or dark-toned background.

Hint: White or other light-toned subjects and back lighting or a bright sky can lead to under exposure—the subject will be too dark. Conversely, black or other dark-toned subjects and backgrounds can lead to over exposure—the subject will be too bright. Check your images on the LCD monitor. If an image would benefit from different flash intensity, set a plus or minus flash exposure compensation and take the photo again (see page 160).

Flash Photography and Camera Exposure Modes

Whether you're using the built-in flash or an accessory unit, you can shoot with any of the camera's available exposure modes. Flash photography with AUTO and the Scene Selection modes was already covered earlier (on page 148) and in Chapter 5, so I will not repeat that information.

Flash Modes

When using the ∝200 in the P, A, S, or M exposure mode, you can select any of three Flash Modes. Press the **Fn** button, scroll to the [Flash Modes] item, press the Controller's center button, scroll to the desired option, and press the center button again to confirm your decision. Any of the following can be used with the built-in flash or a dedicated accessory flash unit.

155

Note: There is no need for a Flash Off mode when using the camera's P, A, S, or M exposure mode; if you do not want the flash to fire, make sure the built-in head is in the down position or that an accessory flash unit is Off.

Fill-Flash ⚡ : The default flash mode, this is suitable for use in bright conditions, such as on a sunny day. The camera's metering system will automatically reduce flash output slightly so the flash provides only "fill" light: to lighten or fill-in shadows. But this mode is also useful when shooting in dark locations; flash will provide the necessary illumination in such conditions.

Slow Sync ⚡SLOW : When this mode is set, the camera will set a slow (long) shutter speed (sync speed) when you're using the P or the A exposure mode. (When you use the S or M mode for flash photography this flash mode has no effect since you are required to set the shutter speed yourself.)

Slow Sync can be useful when taking photos of a nearby subject lit by flash against a distant, not excessively dark, background. For example, use this setting to photograph a person against a nighttime cityscape. The long exposure time will record the ambient light in the scene without affecting the flash exposure. Use a tripod to avoid blur from camera shake and have your subject remain still during the entire exposure.

Rear Sync ⚡REAR : This option refers to rear curtain sync—a feature that causes flash to fire at the end of an exposure, not at the start of an exposure as in conventional flash photography. When used for shooting moving subjects at long shutter speeds (preferably 1/15 second and longer), this feature produces the effect of motion streaks that follow the subject instead of preceding it. Some photographers also use rear sync for long exposures of static objects or people, moving the camera to produce interesting flash blur effects.

Wireless ⚡WL : Select this flash mode only if you own a fully dedicated accessory flash unit and want to use it off-camera without an optional cable to connect the flash unit to the cam-

156

era's hot shoe. (This technique is discussed in detail on pages 166-168). Wireless (also called "remote") flash will work with one or more of the following units: the Sony HVL-AM series and the (discontinued) Maxxum/Dynax HS(D) models.

Exposure Modes

Before moving on to some advanced flash techniques, let's consider basic flash photography—with the built-in flash or a dedicated accessory unit—in the camera's four primary exposure modes.

Program (P): Flash photography in P mode can be quite simple. The camera's metering system controls the shutter speed and aperture used for each shot. (With flash photography, you cannot use the Program shift feature.) The camera also controls the flash output. However, you can set any desired ISO, flash control option, flash mode, and flash exposure compensation (discussed on page 160). When you do so, the ∝200 will not automatically revert to the factory-set defaults when it is turned off or when it goes into Sleep mode, as it does when using the AUTO or Scene modes.

Aperture Priority (A): In A mode when using flash, you select an aperture (f/stop). The aperture used determines the flash range. The maximum flash-to-subject distance decreases with each smaller aperture setting. The chart on page 150 shows the range of the built-in flash. If you're using an accessory flash unit with a data panel, it will provide information about the flash range. The camera will set a shutter speed from 1/60 second to 1/160 second.

When using flash in A mode, the camera will provide a warning if you set an aperture that is likely to produce over-exposure. The shutter speed numeral in the viewfinder will blink before you take a photo. If that happens, set a smaller aperture (such as f/11 instead of f/5.6, for example), or switch to a lower ISO level, until the blinking stops.

The camera does not provide any advance warning in situations where underexposure may occur. If your subject is too far from the flash or a very small aperture is being used, your flash photos may be too dark. (This is less of a problem when using a high-powered accessory flash unit with a great effective flash range.) Check your photo on the LCD monitor; if it is underexposed, set a larger aperture (such as f/5.6 instead of f/16), a higher ISO level, or move closer to the subject. Then, take the shot again.

Shutter Priority (S): When using flash in S mode, you select a shutter speed and the camera will set the aperture. You can set shutter speeds as long as 30 seconds and as short as 1/160 second. The shutter speed cannot exceed that maximum flash sync speed so the camera will not allow you to set a faster shutter speed (except when using the special High-speed Sync feature discussed on pages 169).

Changing the shutter speed will not affect the exposure in conventional flash photography. However, it does allows you to control how ambient light will be rendered. This is especially useful when you have a flash-lit subject in front of a somewhat dark background that you want to be rendered naturally. An example would be your subject in front of a city scene at dusk or a beautiful sunset. If you don't intentionally use a long shutter speed, the picture will probably have a flash-lit subject against a very dark or black background.

Make sure you use a tripod when shooting at long shutter speeds to prevent blur due to camera shake. S mode is also useful when you want to render ambient light motion blurs and a sharp, flash-exposed subject. You should set the camera for Rear sync (see page 164) and use a long shutter speed to capture the ambient exposure of the moving subject. The camera will produce an image with light trails that follow a sharp subject (illuminated by the brief burst of light).

Manual (M): In M mode when using flash, you must set a desired aperture as well as shutter speed. Your shutter speed options are the same as in S mode. Although the camera's M mode is a manual control option, full flash automation is still provided by the light metering system.

Using the camera's Manual mode for flash photography provides more creative control. The photographer can adjust the relationship between the flash and ambient light. In Manual mode, the exposure scale in the ∝200's viewfinder operates, but it only provides a reading for the ambient light in the scene.

If you want the lighting on the subject and the background to be balanced, set the shutter speed and aperture for correct ambient light exposure. If you wish to make an image with a brighter or darker background, you can adjust the shutter speed or aperture. A longer shutter speed provides a brighter background. To set off your subject against a darkened background, use a faster shutter speed or a smaller aperture. (If you close down the aperture, make sure the subject distance is still within the flash range.) Watch the scale in the viewfinder and stop making adjustments when the marker indicates a desired level of difference between subject brightness and background brightness. If the marker on the scale indicates -2 for example, the background will be about 2 EVs or stops darker than the subject illuminated by the flash.

The scale provides data in a +2 to -2 EV range. In many typical conditions, the brightness of the background is not substantially higher or lower than the subject brightness, so the +2 to -2 scale should be adequate. If the background brightness is substantially different than subject brightness—common in very dark locations or with extremely bright backlighting—an arrow at the end of the scale blinks.

Take notice of the flash range, especially when using small apertures; the camera provides no advance warning that the settings in use will underexpose the shot. Check your photo on the LCD monitor. If it's dark, set a larger aperture or a higher ISO. When using one of the compatible accessory flash units with a data panel, you'll find useful information about flash range before taking a photo. It varies depending on the ISO, the aperture that you've selected, and the position of the flash unit's zoom head.

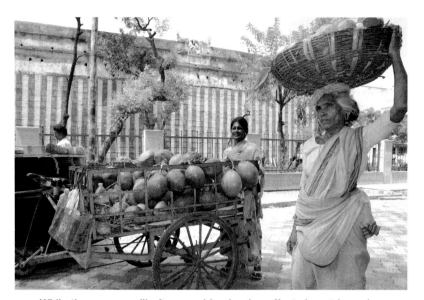

While the camera will often provide pleasing effects in outdoor photography with the ADI or Pre-Flash TTL option, a minus flash exposure compensation level—such as the -2/3 used for this photo—can be useful for a more subtle flash effect.

Modifying Flash Intensity

Regardless of the flash options or shooting techniques used, you may well find that some exposures exhibit more or less flash than you want. After taking any flash photo, review the image on the camera's LCD monitor. If you would prefer a stronger flash or gentler flash effect, simply set flash exposure compensation before taking the shot again.

Flash Exposure Compensation

Particularly in outdoor photography, you may find that you prefer less flash intensity than the system produces at its default. If so, scroll to the [Flash Compens] item in [Recording Menu ☐ 1] and press the Controller's center button. A scale will appear with a pointer at zero, indicating that no flash intensity modification has been set. Scroll to the right (the plus side) to increase flash output or to the left (minus side) to decrease flash output for the subsequent photos that you will take.

This camera feature is effective with the built-in flash and with an on-camera accessory flash unit. (If you also set flash exposure compensation with an accessory unit, that will take precedence over the setting made in the camera.) After you set flash exposure compensation, the ⚡ symbol will appear in the viewfinder as a reminder. Remember to reset this feature to zero when you no longer want to modify flash intensity.

Try setting a -1 flash exposure compensation factor when you want a very subtle flash effect in outdoor photography. Re-shoot and examine the new photo. If it's not quite right, simply access the Flash compensation function and set a slightly different level. Take the photo again. With a bit of experience, you'll become quite adept at judging the amount of minus flash compensation that you might want to use in most situations.

Sometimes, a flash photo will appear underexposed: the subject will be too dark. This can occur when a subject is white (or another very light tone) or is posing against an extremely bright background. When the subject is too dark in a flash photo, try a +1 flash exposure setting and take the shot again. You may need to take several photos, at various compensation levels, to get one image that's technically perfect. Again, with experience, you'll learn to judge the amount of flash compensation that's likely to be suitable.

The ideal amount of flash exposure compensation will vary based on the subject, lighting conditions, and your personal preferences. Note that flash compensation affects only the amount of light output by the built-in or accessory flash. The aperture and shutter speed settings do not change when flash exposure is used, so ambient light exposure is not affected. Only the subject—and not the background—will be lighter or darker in a subsequent flash photo.

Note: The flash exposure compensation feature will have no value if the subject is too close to the camera or too far from the camera. When shooting extreme close-ups, for example, flash intensity may be excessive even after you set a -2 flash exposure compensation level. (In that case, set a lower ISO level and/or move further from the subject.) With a very distant subject, the light from flash may simply not reach adequately far; setting a +2 compensation will have no effect in that case. (In this situation, try setting a higher ISO level and/or moving closer to the subject and/or switching to a high-powered accessory flash unit.)

Using Flash with Exposure Compensation
In some situations, you may prefer to use the camera's conventional exposure compensation control during flash photography. This will modify both the flash exposure and the ambient light exposure. While depressing the [⚡] button, rotate the Control dial [🔆] and set the desired exposure compensation level. (This control is not active while shooting in the camera's M mode, as discussed on page 120 so experiment while shooting in P, A, or S mode.)

Note: The conventional exposure compensation feature is most useful in flash photography when an entire image is too dark or too light. After you set exposure compensation with the [⚡] button, the metering system will adjust the flash exposure as well as the ambient light exposure. If you set a +1 exposure compensation level for example, both the nearby subject and the background will be brighter in the next photo. Conversely, if you set a -1 exposure compensation level, both will be darker in the subsequent photo.

You can also use both types of compensation simultaneously—for modifying flash intensity by a certain level and for modifying the ambient light exposure by another level. For instance, you might set exposure compensation to -1 and flash exposure compensation to +1. That combination would produce a photo with a darker background and a brighter nearby subject. Or, set exposure compensation to +1 and flash exposure to -1 for a photo with a brighter background but a darker nearby subject.

You can achieve any desired effect with this advanced technique, but it does call for a lot of experimentation. Try different levels for each control and check the resulting images on the camera's LCD monitor. With some experience, you'll soon become adept at estimating what settings will produce the most accurate, or creatively pleasing, exposure for the subject and for the background in flash photography.

Other Flash Options

In addition to features already discussed in detail, the ∝200 provides other options for flash photography. Red-eye reduction is available only with the built-in flash. Rear curtain flash sync and slow sync are available with both the built-in flash and dedicated accessory flash units. Two other options, wireless off-camera remote flash control and high speed sync can also be used, but that's possible only with certain accessory flash units.

Red-Eye Reduction ⚡👁

Available in Custom menu 📷 1 , this feature is recommended for use when photographing people or animals in dark locations with the built-in flash. When selected, the flash unit fires several bright bursts intended to reduce the size of the subject's pupils and minimize the red-eye effect. (With pets this is often a blue or green effect, but the cause is the same.) After the pre-flashes, the actual flash burst is fired. This feature is occasionally successful in reducing red-eye but people tend to be annoyed by the bright pre-flashes.

Hint: I do not recommend using Red-eye reduction mode unless you find that the built-in flash produces terrible red-eye in certain circumstances. There are two drawbacks: the bright pre-flashes may cause your subjects to blink or appear unnatural; and there's quite a long delay from the instant that you press the shutter release until the actual exposure is made (during that time, your subjects' expression or position may change).

163

Effective Ways to Reduce Red-Eye:
- Ask the subject not to look directly at the lens.
- Turn up the room lights to cause the iris in the eye to close down, reducing the risk of red-eye.
- Use an accessory flash unit that sits higher above the camera, and hence, further from the lens; the greater flash-to-lens axis distance minimizes red-eye.
- Using an accessory flash unit, bounce the light from a ceiling or wall if your flash unit includes a tilt or swivel head feature.
- Use off-camera flash (see page 166) instead of on-camera flash to maximize the distance between the light source and the lens axis; hold the remote flash unit above and to one side of your subject.
- Use the red-eye correction tool if available with your image editing software program.

Rear Sync 🔆REAR

One of the options available in the Flash Mode item of the Function sub-menu (accessed with the 🔲 button), Rear Sync causes flash to fire at the end of an exposure when the shutter mechanism's second or rear curtain opens. This feature is also called rear curtain or second curtain sync because flash fires just before the second shutter curtain closes. In conventional flash photography, flash fires at the start of an exposure just after the first shutter curtain opens to allow light to reach the CCD sensor.

When used for shooting moving subjects at long shutter speeds (preferably 1/15 second and longer), Rear Sync produces the effect of motion streaks that follow the subject instead of preceding it. Some photographers also use Rear Sync for long exposures of static objects or people, moving the camera to produce interesting flash blur effects.

Motion Blur—How It Works

In order to create motion trails that follow an object, the flash must fire at the end of the exposure, using the Rear sync option. If the flash is fired using the standard flash mode (front curtain sync), the moving object is "frozen" at the beginning of its travel and then the motion trail is recorded. This captures the action but the motion trail appears to be in front of the moving object. However, if the flash fires just before the shutter closes (rear curtain sync), the camera will record the ambient light motion blur and then freeze the subject. Thus, the photo will appear natural, with the motion trail following the object. This technique can produce dramatic action shots, so take the time to experiment with your camera and flash until the effects you want become second nature.

Slow Sync ⚡SLOW

You can set a slow shutter speed (sync speed) such as 1/15 second or 1/4 second while using the camera's S or M mode for flash photography whenever you wish. If you want to take flash photos during a long exposure when using the camera's other modes, set the Slow Sync mode. (It's one of the options in the Flash Mode item of the Function sub-menu accessed with the 🔲 button.) After you do so, the ∝200 will set a longer than usual shutter speed (sync speed) when the built-in or accessory flash is active. (The exact speed depends on scene brightness and the ISO setting.)

This function can be useful when taking photos of a nearby subject lit by flash against a distant, not excessively dark, background. For example, use this setting to photo-graph a person with a nighttime cityscape in the back-ground. The long exposure time will record the ambient light in the scene without affecting the flash exposure. (You can also achieve a similar effect with full camera automation using the Night View Scene Selection mode.) Mount the ∝200 on a sturdy tripod to avoid blurring from camera shake and ask your subject to remain still during the entire exposure which can last for several seconds.

Off-Camera Flash

While on-camera flash is certainly convenient, the ∝200 can be used with an accessory flash unit that's off camera, perhaps held above and to the side of the subject for a more professional lighting effect. That's possible with any dedicated flash unit when using an optional FA-CC1AM Off-Camera Cable to connect the flash unit to the camera's hot shoe. This accessory ensures that full TTL metering and automation are available with one remote flash unit.

The ∝200 also supports off-camera flash without the need for any connecting cable for Wireless remote TTL flash. This feature is available when using one of more of the following units: the Sony HVL-AM series units or the Maxxum/Dynax HS(D)-series. Start by setting the Wireless ⚡WL option in the Flash Mode item under the Function sub-menu (accessed with the **Fn** button). Then, proceed as follows; start by experimenting with the camera in the P, A, or S mode.

Mount the accessory flash in the camera's hot shoe and turn both on; this will activate the Wireless flash feature. Now, remove the accessory flash unit from the camera and pop up the built-in flash head. When you take a photo, the off-camera flash will be triggered by a burst of light from the built-in flash. Metering control is TTL, making it quite easy to get good exposures without any calculations. If you want to use more than one remote flash unit, simply activate the Wireless flash feature with all of the accessory units.

Wireless/Remote Flash Techniques
When the accessory flash unit is charged and ready, its AF illuminator lamp blinks twice, indicating that you can take the photo. The built-in flash will fire a low intensity burst—

Off-camera flash is easy to use and provides several benefits that are
worthwhile even when taking family snapshots. For this photo, I held
an accessory flash unit slightly above and to the side of the girls,
preventing red-eye and the dark shadow that is typical typical with
direct, on-camera flash.

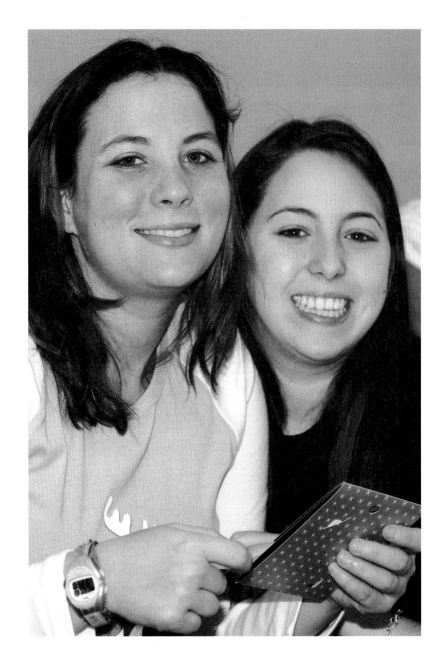

just enough to trigger the remote flash but not enough to light the subject. High-speed sync (HSS; see page 169) can be used in wireless flash photography with the ∝200. Just remember that this feature reduces the effective flash range, especially at very fast shutter speeds.

Initially, practice with a single remote flash unit. If you own two fully compatible flash units, try more advanced setups with one illuminating the subject and the other illuminating the background. Make sure that both remote units maintain the line of sight with the on-camera flash. To be certain, take a test shot.

If your flash photos are too dark or too light, set a plus or minus exposure compensation with the camera's [±] button, or use the accessory flash unit(s)' flash exposure compensation control to increase (plus) or decrease (minus) flash intensity. Remember to reset both controls to zero after they are no longer required.

Flash Range: Wireless flash photography works best indoors, in a location that is not excessively bright. It's important to position the remote flash unit so it's not too close to or too far from the subject.

The distance between the remote flash and your subject should be at least one meter (or 3.3 feet). The maximum distance between flash and subject will vary depending on the power of your flash unit and the ISO level that you set on the camera. It will also vary depending on the aperture you have set on the camera. When shooting at f/5.6, for example with an HVL-56AM flash unit, using ISO 100 and a normal 1/160 second or 1/125 second sync speed, place the flash unit no further than 5 meters (16.4 feet) from the subject. (Additional information on Wireless remote flash range is available with the data sheets packaged with the various Sony flash units.)

Note: To confirm that the built-in flash will trigger the off-camera flash unit(s), press the AEL button. If the Wireless connection is working, all flash units will fire a short burst. After you finish shooting in Wireless mode, be sure to turn this mode off; select one of the other flash modes in the Function sub-menu. If you forget to do so, your exposures (when using the built-in flash) may be incorrect.

High-Speed Sync (HSS)
A feature that's available only with the Sony HVL-AM and the (discontinued) Maxxum/Dynax HS(D)-series flash units, High-speed sync (HSS) mode allows the flash to sync at shutter speeds faster than the normal maximum sync speed (1/160 second). The HSS function is set on the flash unit and allows you to take flash photos at shutter speeds as fast as 1/4000 second. Instead of firing a single burst of light when the shutter is open, HSS mode fires a series of short, lower intensity bursts as the shutter curtain travels across the image plane.

Fast shutter speeds are associated with stopping subject motion, so people may mistakenly think HSS is for photographing moving objects with flash. It is not. This setting is useful when you want to use flash for a subject in bright sunlight, especially with a very wide aperture, such as f/2.8. When using flash at the conventional 1/160 second sync speed, it is likely the image would be overexposed. Using a fast shutter speed controls only the bright ambient light exposure and prevents it from overpowering the flash exposure. By making the photo with a faster sync speed, such as 1/500 second, you can correctly expose for the ambient light and flash.

To utilize HSS, attach one of the specified flash units to the camera's hot shoe and set it to the HSS mode. Note that HSS cannot be used when REAR (Rear sync) or the one of the self-timer options is set on the camera. HSS works in the camera's A, S, and M modes, when you need to use a shutter speed faster than the normal 1/160 second sync speed.

Experiment with HSS on a bright sunny day and set the camera's ISO to 400. Start by using the camera's Shutter Priority (S) mode and try setting a shutter speed of 1/250 second or 1/500 second while the accessory flash unit is on. Or switch to the Aperture Priority (A) mode, set a high ISO on the camera, and select a wide aperture: f/2.8 or f/4; that should cause the metering system to set a fast shutter speed.

If the flash unit includes a data panel, check the information as to flash range; that will change as you or the camera sets different shutter speeds. If the range is not suitable for the camera-to-subject distance, select a different shutter speed and check the data panel again. Setting a higher ISO level in the camera can increase the effective flash range at any shutter speed.

Although you can select shutter speeds as fast as 1/4000 second when using HSS flash, you'll rarely need to use anything faster than about 1/500 second. The flash unit's guide number is dramatically reduced when you use HSS as you select faster shutter speeds in this unconventional flash mode. The flash range also becomes quite short when you select a small aperture (such as f/11 instead of f/4). Unless you're using a very high ISO setting for extreme close-ups in very bright sunshine, a sync speed of 1/250 second to 1/500 second will often be perfect when shooting at wide apertures.

Bounce Flash

Direct flash can often be harsh and unflattering, causing heavy shadows or a "deer in the headlights" appearance in your subject. Bouncing the flash diffuses the light to soften it and create a more natural-looking effect. You can utilize this technique with whether the flash in on- or off-camera.

Most compatible accessory flash units feature heads that are designed to swivel and tilt, although some only allow for tilting upward. Either type can be useful for allowing an on-camera flash to be adjusted so it is not aimed directly at the subject. You can point the flash toward the ceiling at a point

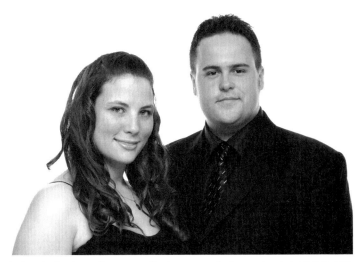

Instead of using off-camera flash, some photographers prefer to use bounce flash, reflecting light from a wall, or usually from a ceiling as in this example. As discussed in the text, bounce flash is not ideal in all respects, but the technique can provide soft, diffused lighting that's quite suitable for some portraits, without the obvious highlights (on the cheek for example) common with other flash techniques. If image contrast is too low, that aspect can be easily corrected afterwards, with Photoshop or other software.

about halfway between the flash and the subject. If the head also swivels, you can point it toward a wall beside the subject. Either technique can produce softer lighting. However, the ceiling and walls must be white or light gray or they may cause an undesirable color cast.

Note: When you bounce flash, the LCD data panel will not show the effective flash range, nor is such data published in owner's manuals—it depends on the distance from the camera to the bounce surface plus the distance to the subject. As a rough estimate, assume that flash range is about half of what it would be with direct flash photography. It can be greater than that if the bounce surface and subject are quite close, or less if the subject and/or the surface is very far from the camera or each other. After taking a photo, check the LCD monitor. If it's too dark, use a wider aperture (such as f/4 instead of f/11) or select a higher ISO level to increase the effective flash range.

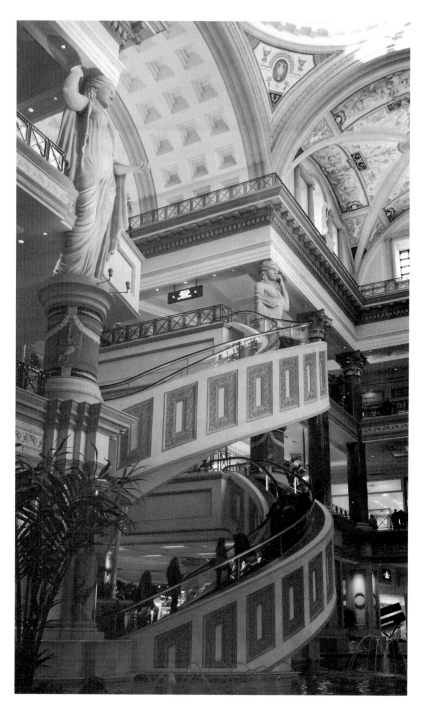

Lenses and Accessories

Sony markets three series of lenses. The Sony G series is multi-platform, meaning it's suitable for all Alpha cameras including the professional model (not yet available at the time of this writing) with an oversized sensor; these lenses are also compatible with the discontinued Maxxum/Dynax 35mm and D-SLR bodies. Somewhat smaller, the DT series was designed exclusively for the Alpha cameras with the typical, smaller sensor size; these are also compatible with the discontinued Maxxum/Dynax D-SLRs.

The Carl Zeiss ZA (Zeiss Alpha) lenses of German design are also multi-platform. These feature a T* designation; that refers to a special multi-layer coating for flare control, proprietary to Carl Zeiss. All of the ZA lenses are high-end optics with large maximum apertures, very rugged construction, and premium-grade optical elements.

Sony does not guarantee that the ∝200 is fully compatible with other brands of lenses, but it should work well with the discontinued Konica Minolta Maxxum/Dynax lenses and with many aftermarket lenses with the Alpha mount. Do note, however, that the Super SteadyShot (anti-shake) system will not work with two Maxxum/Dynax lenses: the 16mm f/2.8 Fisheye and the Zoom 3x–1x f/1.7–2.8 Macro. However, in other respects, those two should be compatible with the ∝200.

While the ∝200 is often purchased in a kit with an inexpensive 18-70mm zoom, Sony markets a wide range of other lenses, including macro, telephoto, and ultra wide. The kit lens is great for getting started but most ∝200 owners will soon want at least one addtional lens for greater versatility or for benefits such as a wider maximum aperture or superior image quality.

Some Maxxum/Dynax lenses, and some aftermarket models with the Alpha mount, are labeled D-type. The D denotes a distance-encoding device (in the lens barrel) that allows the camera to make improved calculation for flash exposure (ADI) when using the built-in flash or an accessory D-series Maxxum/Dynax flash unit. All of the current and future Sony and Carl Zeiss ZA lenses include the distance-encoding device for maximum compatibility with the ∝200, but Sony has not labeled these lenses with the D designation.

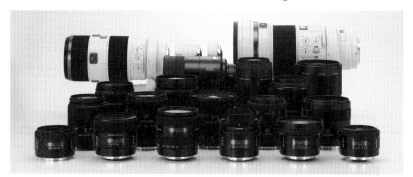

Sony markets a wide range of lenses for the Alpha series of cameras.

Effective Focal Lengths

In the past, the 35mm film frame—measuring 24 x 36 mm in size—was the standard or the norm for most photographers for decades. The vast majority of D-SLR cameras (of all brands) use a sensor that's smaller than that standard. Because of this factor, the field of view with any lens will be narrower than if that same lens were mounted on a 35mm camera.

In the Sony Alpha line, only the professional model will employ an oversized sensor with approximate dimensions of 24 x 36 mm. All of the other Alpha cameras, including the ∝200, are equipped with a 23.6 x 15.8 mm size sensor. That causes field-of-view crop, often called a "focal length magnification factor." In practice, this crop gives the lens a view that has more "telephoto effect" than it would on a 35mm camera.

For comparison purposes, the effective focal length of a lens used on the ∝200 is increased by 1.5x in terms of the field of view that the lens provides. For example, images made with a 20mm lens on the ∝200 will look like images made with a 30mm focal length on a 35mm camera. The 18-70mm zoom (often packaged with the ∝200 in a kit) provides the equivalent of a 27-100mm zoom in 35mm film photography. A 300mm telephoto produces the field of view that we would expect from a 450mm lens.

That's great news if you appreciate sports and wildlife photography; with even a moderate telephoto lens, the ∝ 200 can produce frame-filling images of distant subjects. But it's less than ideal if you prefer wide-angle landscape or travel photography, with images that include scenic vistas. Fortunately, you can find short focal-length lenses such as the Sony 11-18mm f/4.5–5.6 G zoom that produces the view that 35mm film photographers would expect from a 16.5-27mm zoom. In the future, expect to see additional lenses with short focal lengths for ultra wide-angle photography with Alpha cameras, including the ∝200.

Note: Unless otherwise indicated, lenses will be referenced by their actual focal length, not their effective focal length.

Selecting a Lens

Think hard about your specific photographic needs before spending money on lenses. The focal length and design of a lens will have a huge affect on how you photograph. The right lens will make photography a joy; the wrong one will make you leave the camera at home.

One approach is to determine if you are frustrated with your current lenses. Do you constantly want to see more of the scene than the lens will allow? Then consider an ultra-wide-angle lens such as the 11–18mm model. Or maybe the subject is often too small in your photos because it is far from the camera. Then look into acquiring a telephoto lens such as the 75-300mm f/4.5–5.6 model or the newer DT 55-200mm f/4–5.6 zoom.

Portraits look great when shot with focal lengths between 60-90mm with a digital camera such as the ∝200, although some photographers appreciate the effects produced by a slightly longer focal length. Interiors often demand wide-angle lenses. Many people also like wide-angles for land-scapes, but telephotos can come in handy for isolating the most appealing elements of a distant scene.

Normal Lenses

The focal length of a normal lens corresponds to the diago-nal of the format. With 35mm film, this measurement would be exactly 43.3 mm; but for design reasons, most normal lenses for 35mm SLRs are about 50mm. Because of the ∝200's sensor size, a focal length of about 35mm becomes equivalent to the view of a standard lens placed on a 35mm camera. Thus, a lens like Sony's 35mm f/1.4 G, used on the ∝200, becomes a normal lens because it has an effective focal length of 52.5mm (35 mm x 1.5). And a 50mm lens on the ∝200 would have an effective focal length of 75mm, becoming a short telephoto.

With a 35mm focal length lens mounted on the ∝200, subjects in the viewfinder appear about the same size as they look to the naked eye. For most amateur photographers, a normal lens is adequate for many subjects, as long as you get close enough to (or far enough away from) your subject. However, if you want to achieve a closer view without mov-ing physically closer to your subject, for example a horse in a field, you will need to use longer lenses. Conversely, if you want to photograph a sweeping vista or a group of people inside a small room, a shorter focal length will give you a wider field of view.

Telephoto Lenses

Lenses with focal lengths that are greater than a normal lens are called telephotos. In the case of the ∝200, this would be

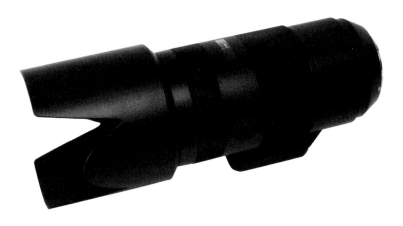

Telephoto zooms are larger and heavier than the more modest 18-70mm "kit" lens; still, most photo enthusiasts buy one because of their versatility.

any lens with a focal length greater than 35mm. They allow us to bring distant subjects "closer." Lenses with focal lengths just beyond normal (35-50mm) are in the short-end range of telephotos.

Telephoto lenses have several interesting characteristics. The longer the focal length, the more obvious these characteristics are. Long lenses compress perspective, reducing the apparent distance between objects in a scene. This is useful for creating interesting effects such as stacking near and distant hills in haze or making a traffic-filled city street look especially congested.

A telephoto's narrow angle of view often limits the number of components that can be included in the image, eliminating clutter. In high magnification photography, depth of field is very shallow, so only the focused plane is sharp; that's useful for blurring away a distracting background, particularly at a wide aperture (small f/number). This makes a telephoto lens an excellent tool for isolating a subject and making it "pop."

Moderate Telephoto Lenses

These are lenses from about 50-135mm on the ∝200. They often feature larger maximum apertures than longer lenses. In the Sony system, lenses of this type include the 50mm f/1.4 G and 135mm f/2.8 G, as well as the Carl Zeiss 135mm f/1.8 ZA model and zooms such as the new (wide angle to moderate telephoto) Carl Zeiss T* 24-70mm f/2.8 ZA. All of these, particularly the Carl Zeiss models, are premium-grade products and are large and heavy due to their wide apertures and rugged construction. Lenses of this type are often regarded as excellent portrait lenses.

Longer Telephoto Lenses

With the ∝200's smaller sensor, even lenses such as the 75-300mm f/4.5–5.6 G zoom or the new high-grade 70-300mm f/4.5–5.6 G SSM zoom will give you quite a bit of reach (450mm equivalent at the long end). Sony also offers larger, pro-caliber telephotos such as the 70-200mm f/2.8 G SSM zoom and the 300mm f/2.8 G SSM model. These boast a very wide maximum aperture that can be useful in low light, allowing the camera to set fast shutter speeds with less need for high ISO levels.

Lenses with focal lengths of 300mm or longer magnify the subject making it easier to produce frame filling photos of distant animals or sports competitors. The increased magnification and size of these lenses can also make camera shake more problematic, but the ∝200's Super SteadyShot stabilizer system is helpful in reducing this.

If you want a lens with an extremely long focal length, the Sony 500mm f/8 G Reflex Mirror lens (750mm equivalent) might be worth considering. It is surprisingly compact and relatively affordable because it employs a different type of technology called "catadioptric," indicating that mirrors extend the light path, making the barrel unusually short. However, the only available aperture is f/8, and that is quite small. Consequently, this lens is not ideal for low light photography unless you are prepared to work at very high ISO levels or use a sturdy tripod to prevent camera shake when shooting at the longer shutter speeds required with f/8.

Wide-Angle Lenses

Wide-angle lenses produce a broad field of view and "expanded spatial perspective." Foreground elements become prominent while more distant objects are "pushed back," rendered smaller than the eye perceives. You can exploit this trait with a variety of subject matter, including cramped interiors, yachts at a marina, or land and cityscapes. Depth of field is also extensive, so an entire vista can be rendered in reasonably sharp focus at almost any aperture.

If you use a focal length of 16mm, with the new DT 16-105mm f/3.5–5.6 zoom for instance, the equivalent focal length becomes 24mm. This provides a wide, almost ultra-wide field of view, that is often ideal for including a large group of people or a panoramic landscape in a single photo. When you want to include even more of a scene into your picture, or while working in limited space where you cannot back up very far, an even wider angle lens may be a better choice. That's why Sony markets the 11-18mm zoom (a 16-27mm equivalent with the ∝200.)

Understanding the Fine Points of Lenses

Lenses focus light rays on a common point: a sensor in a digital camera or film in a conventional camera. But lenses have several other essential functions. They control the amount of light that will make an exposure (using different aperture sizes), the range of acceptable sharpness within a scene (depth of field), the focus, the subject magnification, and the angle of view (the amount of any scene which will be included in the image).

Large vs. Small Maximum Apertures

Some lenses feature a large (wide) maximum aperture such as f/2.8, while others have smaller maximum apertures such as f/5.6. Many zoom lenses have variable maximum apertures. For example, the 75-300mm f/4.5–5.6 G zoom has a maximum aperture of f/4.5 at its short end that diminishes gradually as you zoom to longer focal lengths. By about the 250mm setting, the maximum aperture is f/5.6. By comparison, a pro-caliber zoom, such as the 70-200mm f/2.8 G SSM or the Carl Zeiss 24-70mm f/2.8 model, is very "fast." Its f/2.8 maximum aperture is constant through the zoom range and allows the camera to set faster shutter speeds at any ISO level.

Some lenses—such as the Carl Zeiss 85mm f/1.4 and 135mm f/1.8 ZA models—boast even wider apertures. That can be even more useful, but any wide aperture lens produces a significant tradeoff: much larger size/weight and a substantially higher price than a lens with a more modest maximum aperture. For example, the 75-300mm f/4.5–5.6 G model is far more portable and affordable than the 70-200mm f/2.8 G SSM zoom. That's why most lenses (in all brands of camera systems) feature moderately small to very small maximum apertures; these types outsell the "fast" wide aperture lenses by a very wide margin.

Zoom Lens Pros and Cons

When zoom lenses first came on the market, they were not equivalent to single-focal-length lenses in terms of resolution, color rendition, or contrast. Today, you can get superb image quality from either type.

The best feature of a zoom lens is versatility. A single zoom, such as the DT 18-250mm f/3.5–6.3 model, can replace four or five other lenses, making for greater convenience and portability, but a zoom does have some limitations when compared to single focal length lenses.

The most important drawback to zoom lenses is smaller maximum aperture(s). Except for a few "fast" (f/2.8) professional models, most zooms are slower, featuring smaller maximum apertures. Note too that very few long telephoto zooms feature a very wide maximum aperture such as f/2.8. Consequently, when using the zooms with their smaller max-

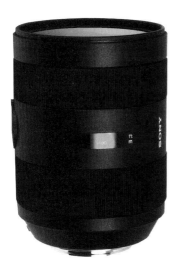

The Carl Zeiss ZA series of lenses are premium grade products with superior optical and mechanical components for pro-caliber image quality and ruggedness.

imum apertures, you'll need to use a higher ISO setting for a fast shutter speed, and the images may exhibit more visible digital noise.

Note: Small maximum aperture is less relevant when shooting with the ∝200, at least in terms of the shutter speeds required to prevent blur from camera shake. When using the Super SteadyShot stabilizer there is less need for fast shutter speeds. Still, in dark locations, and in action photography, the faster shutter speeds available when using a "fast" lens are certainly beneficial.

High-Tech Glass

Some of the wide aperture Sony G and Carl Zeiss ZA telephoto lenses incorporate special glass elements called "low dispersion" or "anomalous dispersion." These modify the way that light rays are bent, producing superior color rendition as well as higher sharpness across the entire image frame. The benefits are most obvious in images made at large apertures and long focal lengths.

An increasing number of wide-angle lenses, including some of the Sony and Carl Zeiss models incorporate element(s) with a non-spherical surface. Such "aspherical" glass can minimize flare while providing more consistent sharpness across the frame at large apertures, and less bending of straight lines near the edges of the image. A single aspherical element can take the place of two conventional elements, reducing size and weight of the lens.

Ultrasonic Focusing Motor

Several of the Sony G lenses are designated as SSM, for Super Sonic wave Motor, indicating an ultrasonic focus motor. The primary advantages are quieter operation and excellent starting/stopping response. These provide the fastest autofocus possible with the ∝200 and the other Alpha cameras. As a bonus, they also allow for manual focus adjustment without the need to switch the camera to manual focus. That can be useful for slight focus touch-ups when the AF system does not focus on the most important subject area, such as the eyes in a portrait photo.

ADI Compatibility

All of the Sony G and Carl Zeiss ZA lenses (as well as D-series Konica Minolta Maxxum/Dynax lenses) incorporate a distance encoding chip that is required for full compatibility with ADI (Advanced Distance Integration) flash metering. This metering system is less influenced by subjects of high reflectance (such as a bride in a white gown) or low reflectance (such as groomsmen in black tuxedos). By combining subject distance into the equation for a correct flash exposure, the ADI system can produce better results when using the built-in flash or a fully compatible accessory flash. (When a conventional Maxxum/Dynax lens is used, the camera employs the older, conventional Pre-Flash TTL metering as discussed in the previous chapter.)

Digital Optimization

All of the Sony G and Carl Zeiss Alpha lenses (as well as discontinued Maxxum/Dynax D-series lenses) are optimized for use with a D-SLR camera. Digital optimization minimizes vignetting (darkening at the corners), maximizes sharpness near the edges of the frame, and prevents internal reflections that can cause flare. These are especially advantageous when using wide-angle lenses at their widest available apertures.

As mentioned on page 173, the Sony G and Carl Zeiss ZA lenses fall into the multi-format category while the DT series was designed exclusively for use with a D-SLR such as the ∝200. Both types are digitally optimized. Do not use a Sony DT lens (or one of the discontinued Maxxum/Dynax DT lenses) on a 35mm Maxxum/Dynax camera or on the Sony Alpha pro camera with its huge sensor; if you were to do so, the corners of the image would be black. That's because the smaller DT-series lenses do not project an image circle that covers the larger 35mm film frame or the professional camera's oversized sensor.

Close-Up Photography

Some Sony telephoto zoom lenses allow for close focusing in order to render a small subject about 1/4 life-size on the image sensor (also called 0.25x magnification, or a 1:4 reproduction ratio). However, Sony also makes true macro lenses that produce a life-size rendition (1:1 reproduction ratio) at the closest focusing distance. Thus, a honey bee will be exactly bee-sized on the digital sensor, without the need for magnification.

Sony offers two true macro lenses: the 50mm f/2.8 G and the 100mm f/2.8 G. The longer macro lens is most useful in nature photography because it provides high magnification at a greater focusing distance. This eliminates the need to be extremely close to a skittish subject, such as a butterfly.

If you don't own a lens that allows for extremely close focusing and you cannot justify the cost of a true macro lens, check out two types of devices that are available.

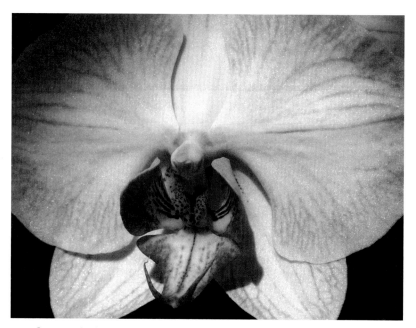

Some telephoto zoom lenses are "macro" designated, indicating close focusing ability. True macro lenses, however, can focus to much shorter distances and also provide superior image quality.

Magnifying Filters: Resembling magnifying glass in a filter mount, a "close-up filter" or "plus diopter" is ideal for use with telephoto zoom lenses. Simply screw it into the front threads of the lens as you would with any type of filter. This type of accessory is not available from Sony but is sold by various filter manufacturers. For the best image quality, look for models that are "achromatic" (highly-corrected, multi-element lenses).

Extension Tubes: Available from aftermarket manufacturers, extension tubes are hollow tubes without any optical elements. They fit between the lens and the camera, and move the optical center of the lens farther from the sensor. This allows the lens to focus much closer than it could normally. Automatic extension tubes (dedicated to Maxxum/Dynax cameras and hence to the Sony camera) maintain the camera's automatic functions. They are designed to work with all lenses for your ∝200, but are most suitable for fixed focal length lenses that are 50mm or longer.

Be aware that extension tubes do cause a considerable light loss and, in general, should only be used with a camera that is on a tripod or other support. The camera's light metering system compensates for this loss of light by selecting a longer shutter speed, but with longer tubes, you may need to use a higher ISO setting.

Hint: Though relatively expensive, true macro lenses are a good investment for anyone who often needs extremely close focusing capability. Such lenses are designed for superb sharpness at all distances and will focus from mere inches to infinity. In addition, they are typically optimized for flat-field photography. If you do not often need that capability, buy a quality close-up filter for a zoom lens or a 25mm extension tube for a 50mm or longer single focal length lens.

Whether using a macro lens or accessories, depth of field is extremely shallow at close distances. The range of acceptable sharpness may be only a centimeter or two. Anything outside the depth of field will be unsharp to some extent. Do not confuse this effect with poor optical quality. For greater depth of field, use a small aperture such as f/16. Focus manually, with extreme care, on the most important subject element: the eyes of an insect, for example. After taking a shot, review it on the LCD monitor, using the magnify feature; if the focus or depth of field is not correct, re-shoot after modifying focus or selecting a smaller aperture.

Due to the higher magnification at extremely close focus, even the slightest camera movement or subject movement will produce an unsharp image. Use a tripod and an ISO setting that will provide a moderately fast shutter speed of at least 1/125 second, if possible.

Other Lens Accessories

Teleconverters

A teleconverter is an optical attachment consisting of a group of elements in a tubular mount. It is placed between the camera body and the lens, and it effectively increases the focal length of the lens in use.

Inexpensive versions are available from aftermarket manufacturers, but Sony offers two premium quality teleconverters for the ∝200: the 14 TC and the 20 TC. The 14 TC extends a lens' focal length by a factor of 1.4x, and the 20 TC does the same by a factor of 2x. They are an alternative to the steeper investment often required to purchase top-quality telephoto lenses.

Both of these converters are compatible with the Sony 70-200mm f/2.8 G SSM, Sony 300mm f/2.8 G SSM, and certain others such as the Sony 135mm f/2.8 STF lenses. In addition, they can be used with the discontinued Maxxum/Dynax APO G-series of fixed focal length lenses ranging from 200mm to 600mm.

While increasing the reach of your telephoto or zoom lens, be aware that teleconverters reduce the amount of light that reaches the image sensor. A 1.4x converter will cause a 1-stop loss of light, while a 2x leads to a 2-stop loss.

Protective Filters

Some photographers buy haze or skylight filters to protect the front lens element from scratches. After all, a filter is less expensive to replace than a damaged lens element. A protective filter can also be useful in such conditions as strong wind, rain, blowing sand, or when going through brush. If you do use a filter for lens protection, a high-quality filter is best, preferably one that is multi-coated to reduce flare. An inexpensive filter can degrade image quality. Remove any filter when shooting toward the sun to minimize the risk of flare.

Graduated Filters

Because the color balance of an image can be controlled by white balance settings, photographers rarely need color balancing filters. A filter that is useful in digital photography is a graduated neutral density filter, or ND grad. Half of the filter is clear while the other half is dark (gray.) It is often used in landscape or cityscape photography to reduce bright areas (such as sky), while not affecting darker areas (such as the ground).

Square or rectangular ND grad filters are convenient. When used with a filter holder designed for them, these filters can be moved up and down until the center lines up with the horizon in the scene.

Polarizing Filters

I strongly recommend the circular polarizer, preferably a multi-coated model of high optical quality. By blocking polarized light reflected from water droplets and particles in the air, this accessory can deepen the tone of a blue sky. A polarizer also reduces glare from non-metallic subject surfaces for richer, more saturated colors.

Note: There are two types of polarizers, "circular" and "linear." They look identical and produce the same result but use different technology. The ∝200 requires a circular polarizer for correct exposure and accurate autofocus.

As you rotate the polarizer, watch the effect—richer sky colors for example—through the camera's viewfinder. A polarizer works best when the sun is at a 90° angle to your position. If the sun is directly behind you, or if you are shooting directly into the light, a polarizer won't have any effect. But if the sun is to the side, or directly overhead, the filter will work its magic effectively.

Lens Hood

Sometimes called a lens shade, this short tube attaches to the front of the lens and reduces glare by blocking undesirable light from reaching the lens. It also offers protection to the front of the lens.

Camera Support Accessories

If you want to get the most from your Sony camera and lenses, be aware that camera movement affects sharpness significantly, causing image blurring. While the anti-shake system allows us to use longer shutter speeds in hand-held shooting, it cannot perform miracles. A rigid tripod is an essential accessory when you cannot use fast shutter speeds, when shooting with longer telephoto lenses, and for close-up work. By holding the camera/lens rock steady, it can assure sharp images.

Hint: When the camera is mounted on a tripod, consider using an electronic cable release. Two models are available: the Remote Commander RM-S1AM with a cable length of 19.75 inches (0.5 meters), and the longer RM-L1AM with a cable of 39.5 inches (1 meter).

When using a cable release, you can set the camera's self-timer for a 2-second delay, although that technique does not allow for taking a shot at the perfect instant in sports and wildlife photography.

Tripods are the most commonly used camera stabilizing device, but beanbags, monopods, mini-tripods, shoulder stocks, and clamps can be useful too. Many photographers carry a small beanbag or a clamp pod for those situations where a tripod isn't practical. A good tripod is an excellent investment. A cheap tripod can actually be wobbly and cause more problems than it solves. When buying a tripod, extend it all the way to see how easy it is to open, then lean on it to see how stiff it is. Both aluminum and carbon-fiber tripods offer great rigidity. Carbon-fiber is much lighter, but also more expensive.

The tripod head is an important consideration and may be sold separately. There are two basic types for still photography: the ball head (my favorite) and the pan-and-tilt head. Both designs are capable of solid support. The biggest difference between them is how you loosen the controls and

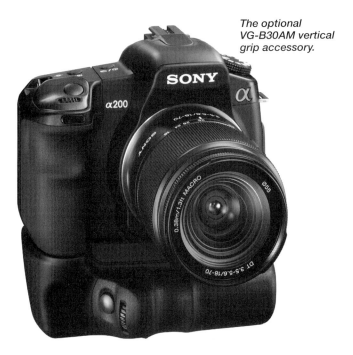

adjust the camera. Try both and see which seems to work better for you. Be sure to do this with a camera on the tripod because that added weight changes how the head works.

Vertical Battery Grip

The ∝200 is compatible with a new accessory, the VG-B30AM vertical grip, which makes using the camera in a vertical (portrait) orientation particularly convenient. This accessory is equipped with a secondary shutter release button and other controls. It accepts two of the NP-FM500H batteries although you can use only one if desired; when two batteries are inserted, the camera will employ one of them, switching to the other as necessary, allowing you to shoot up to 1500 photos before recharging. An optional STP-GB1AM hand strap is also available for this grip accessory, providing extra stability.

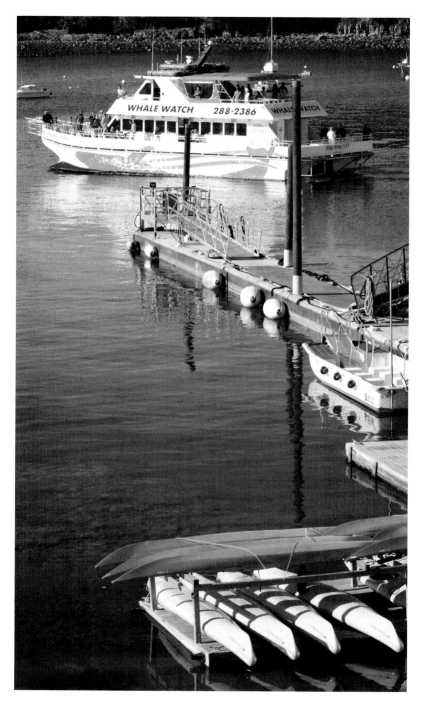

Working with Images

Taking great pictures with your ∝200 is only one component of the digital photography experience. You may also want to download images to a computer, convert RAW files, file and store your photos for easy access and viewing, enhance them using image processing programs, and make prints.

Image Data

A wealth of information is recorded when you shoot a digital picture with the ∝100. This data is stored in the Exchangeable Image File Format (EXIF—often called by the generic term of Metadata).

This EXIF data embedded with the image file includes: date and time of recording, aperture, shutter speed, ISO, exposure mode, metering mode, lens focal length, white balance setting, color mode, exposure or flash compensation, and settings for color saturation, contrast, or sharpness. Some of this information will be used by the printer in direct printing, as discussed on page 203.

You can examine some of the EXIF data on the camera's LCD monitor in Playback mode, by pressing the DISP button twice. You can also review all of the data using the Sony software or other brands of imaging programs. It's worth occasionally checking all of the data as a reminder of the camera settings that you used. Compare pictures and data to learn more about exposure, depth of field, the depiction of motion, flash exposure, and so on.

☞ *In both RAW and JPEG capture modes, your ∝200 records a wealth of data about settings used to make the images, including the f/stop, shutter speed, ISO, exposure mode, any overrides, and so on. By studying this data while viewing a series of images on a computer monitor, you can learn a great deal about how settings affected the look of your photos.*

191

Downloading Images

There are two main ways of getting digital files off the memory card and into your computer. One is to use an accessory card reader that downloads the files from your card. Another is to download images directly from the memory card in the camera using the USB cable included with your ∝200. Direct downloading eliminates the need to buy a card reader, but it means you have to get your cable and connect (then disconnect) the camera to the computer each time you want to download. By contrast, a card reader simply remains connected to your computer and ready for use at all times. Also, downloading directly from the camera consumes a great deal of battery power, which is one argument for using optional AC Adapter AC-VQ900AM.

Card readers allow you to download images to your computer without using the camera.

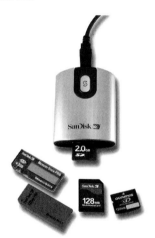

Memory Card Reader

A memory card reader is a simple desktop device that plugs into your computer either using a USB or FireWire connection. Card readers usually read one particular type of memory card, or can be designed to accept several different kinds of cards. The latter can be useful if you use both Memory Stick Duo cards (with an adapter) and CompactFlash cards with your ∝200, or if you also own another digital camera that uses a memory card of some other format.

After you have connected the card reader to your computer, put the memory card into the appropriate slot. The card should appear as an additional drive on current Windows and Mac operating systems; for other operating systems you may need to first install the drivers that come with the card reader. Select your files from the card reader and drag them to a preferred computer drive and folder.

PC Card Adapter

If you use a laptop, especially when traveling, you may prefer an alternative to the card reader known as a CompactFlash to PC card adapter. (Some computer manufacturers equip their laptop machines with a CompactFlash card reader, eliminating the need for the adapter.) The adapter device is compatible with any laptop's PC card slot. Insert the memory card into the CompactFlash to PC card adapter. Then, insert the adapter into your laptop's PC card slot. The computer will recognize this as a new drive, and then you can drag and drop images from the card to the desired folder in your computer's hard drive.

Hint: Most CompactFlash to PC card adapters use the 16-bit standard, but several companies make 32-bit PC card adapters, sometimes called Cardbus 32 Adapters. These can take advantage of internal bus speeds that can be four-to-six times faster. The 32-bit accessory costs three or four times more, but it's great when you have large image files to download to a laptop computer.

Direct from the Camera

Make sure to use either a fully charged battery or the optional Adapter AC-VQ900AM. Turn the camera on to make sure the [USB Connection] item in [Setup Menu 2 ⚒ 2] is set for [Mass storage] (see page 98). Now, be sure to turn the camera off before taking the next steps.

Note: You must use a computer with a USB port and USB interface support. USB connectivity must be installed if your computer does not include it. Also, your PC must use Windows ME, 2000, XP (SP2), Vista, or Apple's Mac OS 10, version 10.1.3 or later. If you own a computer with a Mac OS X operating system, you can download images from the camera but you will not be able to use the Sony Picture Motion Browser, because it is not Mac compatible. For additional specifics about compatibility, check the latest information available at www.sony.net; after reaching that page, select your geographic area.

With the ∝200 powered off, plug the supplied USB cable into the terminal under the card slot cover on the right side of the camera. Plug the other end into your computer's USB port; to prevent possible problems, do not attach to a USB hub. Turn the camera on and look at the LCD monitor to confirm connection. Data transfer will then begin.

Caution: Never disconnect the camera or switch to a different memory card while the camera's red access lamp is lit. If you do, data will be lost and the memory card may be permanently damaged.

If you're using Windows XP or Mac OS X, a window may appear on your computer monitor designed for downloading images; follow the instructions it provides. An icon should also appear designating the camera as a drive, for example, "Removable Disk (D:)." If the latter does not appear, disconnect the camera and start the process over.

With Windows-based computers, the Sony Picture Motion Browser should launch automatically; you can then designate the folder in your computer where the images should be sent. With Mac computers, you will need to drag and drop images from the DCIM folder to the desired folder in your computer. You can do the same with Windows-based computers if you do not use the automated Picture Motion Browser feature.

Double click on the DCIM folder to reveal the specific files in the folder. (The "Misc" folder contains data that may be required for DPOF printing, discussed later in this chapter.) Do not change the names of any folder or file. To copy images, simply drag and drop the file icons to a location in your computer, such as "C: My Pictures." Be sure to specify Copy instead of Move.

A .jpg suffix indicates a JPEG image, which can be read and manipulated by nearly all imaging programs. The .arw suffix indicates a RAW file. You can download these, but later you'll need to use special software to convert them to another format, most likely JPEG, or (preferably) to TIFF. (To use Sony's Image Data Converter SR, you need Windows ME, 2000, or XP for PCs; with a Mac you must be running OS X 10.1.3 or later). You can also use other RAW-compatible programs, such as Adobe Lightroom, Photoshop CS3, or Adobe Elements 5.0 (or later versions of each).

Note: If your copy of the relevant Adobe software does not support the ARW format files generated by the ∝200, you will need to download from Adobe's website a newer version of the Adobe Camera Raw plug-in; be sure to install the plug-in exactly as specified by Adobe.

After downloading is complete, the red access lamp on back of the ∝200 will go out. Switch the camera off and disconnect the USB cable. If your Windows system requires that you first "Stop Mass Storage Device," be sure to follow the "Unplug" or "Eject" hardware routine before unplugging the camera or switching to a new memory card. If using a Mac computer, drag the mass storage device icon for the camera into the trash.

When finished, turn off the camera and unplug it. If you only want to download files from another memory card, do not disconnect the camera, just turn it off. Then change memory cards and turn the camera on again to reestablish the USB connection.

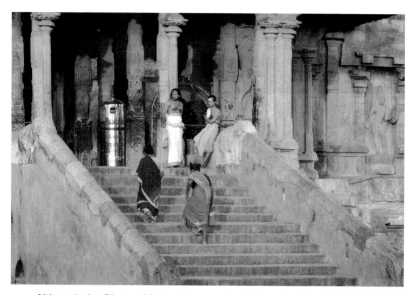

Although the Picture Motion Browser includes a few tools for image enhancement, it's not intended as an alternative to the very versatile aftermarket image-editing programs. Still, if a JPEG requires only minor tweaking, the Sony program can be useful (for those who own a Windows-based computer.)

Bundled (Included) Software

Picture Motion Browser

Compatible only with Windows ME, 2000, XP (SP2) and Vista, but not with Mac operating systems, this is an uncomplicated program that includes a basic browser and a few essential image adjustment options. (A full Help menu is available when you click on Help, or the menu icon at the top of the screen.) Full (EXIF) shooting data can be displayed by right clicking on an image that's displayed in the browser screen and selecting Image information.

Picture Motion Browser possesses a variety of image-enhancing tools, including Auto Correction plus others, for adjusting attributes such as brightness, sharpness, tone curves, and color saturation, as well as a red-eye removal. It also allows you to adjust, rotate, crop, and print your JPEG images. It's not compatible with ARW format files, but you can specify that you want to open these files with other software.

Image Data Converter SR

Compatible with both Windows and Mac operating systems, the Image Data Converter SR can be used to enhance your ARW format RAW files and convert them to JPEG or to TIFF. This program also includes many tools for adjusting brightness, contrast, hue, white balance, and so on. Experiment with the various tools until you get the color and exposure adjusted to your liking before converting the ARW file. Be aware that extensive adjustment is a slow process, because it takes several seconds for each change to be applied to the image.

Take care to avoid loss of important highlight or shadow detail. Set contrast, color saturation, and sharpness at fairly low levels because it's easy to boost these factors using image-processing software after you've converted from ARW; it's much more difficult to moderate or tone down excessively high levels.

After the enhancement is finished, convert and save your image file in an appropriate file folder in your computer. After you click Save As, select the 8-bit option unless you own a program with full support for 16-bit TIFF files. Be sure to give each image a unique name instead of using the more meaningless file name assigned by the camera. Afterwards, you can further fine-tune or manipulate the converted image using your image-processing software.

Browser and Image-Editing Software

Browser programs allow you to look at and organize photos on your computer. They often include additional functions to help you manage your stored image files, such as the ability to search for files, rename photos (either one at a time or in a batch), move image files to different storage locations, resize photos for e-mailing, create simple slideshows, and more.

Sony's Picture Motion Browser is a basic browser that can help organize photos. It's not compatible with Mac operating systems, and it is not as versatile as some programs specifically made for this purpose. You can find a number of such browsers for purchase. For example, the latest version of ACDSee software is a superb program with a customizable interface and such features as a calendar that lets you find photos by date. Another very good program with similar capabilities is CompuPic. And Digital PhotoPro was designed by professional photographers and includes some interesting pro features, like a magnifying digital "loupe."

An important function of a superior browser program is its ability to print customized index prints. You can then give a title to each of these index prints, and list additional information such as your name and address, as well as the photo's file location. The index print serves as a hardcopy that can be used for easy reference (and visual searches). You might want to include index prints with every backup CD or DVD you burn so you can quickly reference what is on the backup and easily find the file you need. A combination of uniquely labeled file folders on your hard drive, a browser program, and index prints will help you to maintain the quickest and most efficient way of finding and sorting images.

Note: Some browser programs may allow you to view the ARW format RAW files generated by the ∝200, but they cannot convert the files into another format. Do not attempt to open or to modify an ARW format file with any software that was not specifically designed for that purpose. Some of the more versatile image editing software programs (including the Adobe products mentioned) include ARW-format converters. These may be faster than Image Data Converter SR, but should be used only if they are compatible with the ARW format files generated by the ∝200.

After converting your ARW format RAW files to JPEG or TIFF, you can use any brand of image-processing software to further enhance them. These programs usually have tools to perform a number of additional functions like cloning and layers, so it may be a good idea to consider owning such a full-featured program. Examples include the latest versions of Adobe Photoshop, Elements, and Lightroom; Apple Aperture and Paint Shop Pro; Microsoft Digital Image Suite; or Ulead PhotoImpact, to name a few.

Note: Check the software distributor's website frequently for updates to see if your imaging software supports the ARW format RAW files generated by the ∝200. Once you see it is supported, download and install the update to view, open, adjust, and convert ARW files.

Image Cataloging

If you prefer not to use a browser program that organizes your image files, how can you edit and file your digital images so that they are accessible and easy to use? One way is to create specific folders for groups of images in your computer's hard drive. For example, in "C:MyPictures," you might create a variety of folders with titles like Vacation 2008, Tom's Graduation, Louisa's Birthday, and so on. Create new folders frequently for new events or new subject matter such as Trip to India, Puerto Rico, or Kate's Florida Birds. You can organize your photo folders alphabetically or by date inside a "parent" folder.

Before downloading any images to your computer, take a few minutes to review them on the camera's LCD monitor. Delete any that are obviously unacceptable, keeping those you want to look at more closely. After downloading these remaining photos, review them again on your computer monitor. Erase any additional images that you do not want in order to avoid squandering precious hard drive space.

Rename the images with descriptive file names. You will probably agree that "Erin_BDay_Candles.jpg" makes more sense as a file name than DSC4519.jpg, for example. Later, be sure to convert any JPEG files to TIFF before enhancing with image-editing software. Processing and resaving JPEG files in a computer can cause image degradation; that is also an argument for converting your ARW format RAW files to TIFF instead of to JPEG.

Hint: After shooting an event, you may want to set up one folder for the images: Paul and Janet's Wedding, for example. After you adjust a photo using image-processing software, save it using a different file name. If the file name was "Bridesmaids_4.tif," for example, you might save the enhanced file as "Bridesmaids_4B.tif." This step will prevent overwriting of the original image so you can later return to it and try entirely different enhancing effects, or use more sophisticated image-processing software.

Image Storage

Although your images are stored as digital files, they can still be lost or destroyed without proper care. You will need a good back-up system. Many photographers use two hard drives, either adding a second one to the inside of the computer or using an external USB or FireWire drive. This allows them to easily back up photos on the second drive. It is very rare for two drives to fail at once.

However, you should also burn your images to CDs or DVDs. Hard drives, zip discs, and memory cards are certainly useful devices, but they are not ideal for long-term storage. The life of a hard drive is unknown, but hard drive failures can occur after a couple of years, not to mention accidental erasure. And a number of malicious computer viruses can wipe out image files from a hard drive (especially JPEGs).

The answer to these storage problems is optical media. A CD and/or DVD-writer (or "burner") is a necessity for the digital photographer. DVDs can store about eight times the data that can be saved on a CD. Either option allows you to back up photo files and store images safely.

Hint: For long-term storage of images, only use R discs. The storage medium used for CD-R and DVD-R discs is more stable than rewriteable media such as RWs. If disc permanence is important, look for CD-R or DVD-R discs that are rated as archival, such as the Mitsui Gold, the new Kodak Professional Grade (gold), or Delkin e-Film Archival Gold products.

Video Output

The ∝200 can also be connected to a television set, allowing you to show JPEG images to friends and family in a convenient manner. If you decide to try this feature, start by making sure that the Video output option in [Setup Menu 1 ↘ 1] is set for the correct TV standard, [NTSC] (North America) or [PAL] (Europe and most other regions of the world).

Turn off the television or the VCR as well as the camera. Insert one end of the video cable (provided with the camera) to the Video Out terminal under the cover for the memory card slot. (It's the same port that's used for USB.) Plug the other end into the video input terminal of the TV or VCR. Turn the video device(s) on and select the video channel. Turn the camera on and press the playback button.

Images will be displayed on the TV instead of the LCD, as they would in conventional camera Playback mode.

Printing

Direct Printing

You can also use the ∝200 for direct printing without using a computer. This feature is available when you connect the camera to a PictBridge compatible photo printer using the USB cable provided with the camera. It works only with JPEG images and only those made in one of the sRGB Color Modes.

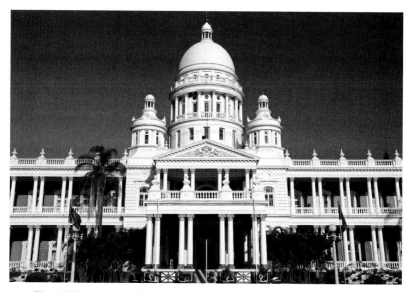

The A200 is compatible with both PictBridge and DPOF technology. That allows for making photos direct from the camera with a PictBridge compliant printer or providing advance instructions that will be followed by a DPOF compliant printer.

Note: PictBridge is a technology that allows for direct printing between a digital camera and printer as long as both are PictBridge compliant. The ∝200 is PictBridge compatible, as are most Epson, Canon, and HP photo printers released since 2004. Look for the PictBridge logo on the printer's box. Some photo printers also include slots for memory cards, allowing you to print JPEGs directly from the camera's memory card; this method does not require a PictBridge compliant printer.

Start with a fully charged camera battery or use the optional AC Adapter. Make sure that the USB connection item in [Setup Menu 2 ✎ 2] is set to [PTP]. Turn the camera off and connect the USB cable from the camera to the printer. Then turn the camera on. The PictBridge screen will appear on the LCD monitor. Use the Controller keys to scroll

and identify the image to be printed and to select the number of copies to be made. You can also activate or close the
PictBridge menu using the camera's MENU button.

You can control the entire printing process using the Controller keys to make an index print of all images on the
memory card, select the paper size, layout, and print quality,
make printer setup changes, and so on. Finally, select
Print>OK in the menu and press the Controller's central button to proceed with the printing.

Direct printing will not give you the same results as printing from images that have been enhanced in a computer
using image-editing software because you have far fewer
options to adjust image aspects such as color, contrast,
brightness, and sharpening. The amount of control you have
over the photo is limited entirely by the printer. Some printers do allow minimal image enhancement during direct
printing, while others offer none at all.

Digital Print Order Format (DPOF)
Another printing feature of the ∝200 is DPOF: Digital Print
Order Format. This allows you to decide which JPEG images
to print before you actually do any printing. (RAW files cannot be identified for DPOF printing.) Then, if you (or your
photo lab) have a DPOF compliant printer, it will print those
selected JPEGs after you make the USB connection. The
DPOF options are available in [Playback Menu 1 ▶ 1] (see
page 93) and include [Marked images], [All images] and
[Cancel all].

Use the Marked images option and identify the images
you want to print using the left/right keys of the Controller;
select the number of prints (from 1 to 9) you'll want of each
image with the ⊕ or ⊖ buttons. Then press the
MENU button, scroll to OK, and press the Controller's center
button to confirm your decision.

Other Printing Options

Unless they own a fully equipped darkroom, photographers who still use 35mm must leave their film at a photofinisher for processing and printing. After a period of time passes, they must return to the store to pick up the order. With digital photography, images can be printed immediately after taking the picture. There are multiple choices for printing. The following are most common:

Computer Download: After downloading images to a computer, use your own photo printer to make prints of any desired image.

Direct-Print Printers: Use a photo printer with a card reader (slots for memory cards) to make prints directly from the JPEGs on your card. Many such machines provide some control over exposure, color rendition, and cropping. Or, hook up your camera to a PictBridge compliant printer to make prints from the memory card in the camera.

Kiosks: Many stores offer self-service photo kiosks—just plug your memory card into the slot. Use the kiosk's controls to crop and enhance JPEG images from your memory card; specify the desired size and quantity.

Photofinishers and Mini-Labs: Most photo labs now have the capability to take your memory card and make prints or CDs from the image files.

On-Line Services: There are many photofinishers that offer their services through websites. Prices are reasonable and your prints are delivered by mail. Once you start an online album on a company's website, you can invite friends and relatives to view images and order prints.

Many surverys confirm that only a small percentage of digital images are ever printed. That's surprising, considering the relative simplicity and low cost of getting beautiful photo prints using some of the methods discussed in the text.

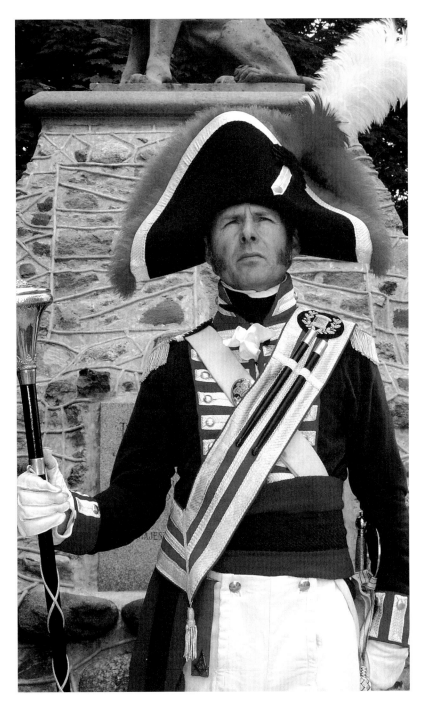

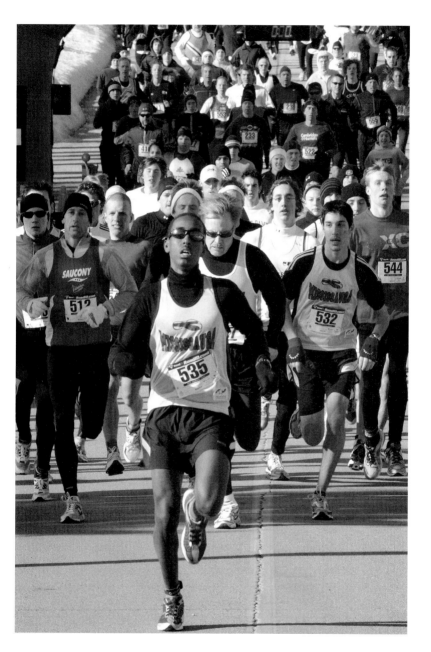

Troubleshooting Guide

The Sony Alpha ∝200 is a sophisticated camera that provides reliable service. Although rare, a malfunction can occur as with any electronic device. And occasionally an inappropriate camera setting can lead to a technical problem. The following chart provides steps you can take in such cases.

Note: Unlike some cameras, the ∝200 does not include a reset button for use in case of some electronic malfunction. (The Reset items in the menu are strictly for resetting features to the factory-recommended defaults.) However, removing the battery (or unplugging the optional AC adapter) for 30 seconds achieves the same purpose. Do not remove the battery (or disconnect the AC adapter) when the red recording lamp on the camera back is lit; if you do so, the images may be corrupted and, in a worst-case scenario, the memory card may be damaged.

Web Support

Check the Sony Web site (www.sony.net, then select your geographic area) occasionally for updates to firmware (in-camera software), new tips on problem solving, or information on company authorized service centers in your area. The following recommendations should solve most problems; however, if you experience camera malfunction—especially one that cannot be solved by removing the battery for 30 seconds—contact an authorized service center.

↶ *Like any complex piece of electronic equipment, the ∝200 may occasionally create frustration; usually, the problem is quite easy to solve using the hints provided in this chapter.*

Problem	Solution
Cannot install battery	Make sure you are inserting it in the proper orientation.
Camera does not turn on	Make sure the battery is charged and properly installed.
Battery life is very short	Ensure that you charge the battery fully as discussed on page 38. If shooting in low temperatures, warm the battery (under your coat or indoors) and try again. In other conditions, gently clean the battery terminals with a soft cloth. If the problem persists, the battery may need to be replaced.
Camera shuts down unexpectedly	See above re: battery. Also remember that the α200 goes into sleep mode after a period of non-use, to conserve battery power. Touch the shutter release button to re-activate it.
Nothing is displayed on the LCD monitor	Press the display button |O| . Make sure nothing is near the camera's eye-piece activating the Eye-Start system; when the latter is active, the LCD display turns off automatically.
The viewfinder image is not sharp	Adjust the eyepiece diopter control to suit your vision.
The camera will not take photos	Make sure the lens is mounted prop-erly. Make sure a memory card is loaded. See if the memory card is full; delete some unwanted images or insert a new card. If using a Memory Stick Duo card, make sure the write-protect switch is set to the Recording (not the Lock) position. Remember too that in some modes, the camera will not fire if the autofocus system is unable to confirm focus. Use manual focus if necessary.

Problem	Solution
The autofocus does not work	Make sure the AF/MF switch is set to AF. If extremely close to your subject, try moving farther. In very dark conditions, the AF system may have difficulty finding focus; try manual focus.
The flash does not work	Make sure the built-in unit is in the up position or that an accessory unit is ON. Flash will not fire in bright conditions in certain operating modes as discussed on pages 157-160; switch to another mode such as P.
Flash photos are too dark	You may be beyond the range of the flash. Move closer and/or set a higher ISO level. If you are not far from the subject, try setting a +1 flash exposure compensation level in Recording Menu ◘ 1 for greater flash intensity.
The bottom of flash photos are dark	In close-focusing, the lens barrel can block some of the light from the built-in flash; move farther from the subject. Try removing the lens hood.
The flash takes a long time to recycle	This is common after shooting several flash photos in sequence.
Numerals in the viewfinder are blinking	The scene may be too dark or too bright for a proper exposure at the selected settings. Try setting a different (aperture) f/stop or shutter speed until the blinking stops or try setting a different ISO level.
Images are too dark	When you take photos of a light-toned subject or shoot toward a bright area, some plus-exposure compensation may be required; set that using the ☒ button and the camera's ▲ dial.
Images are too bright	You may need to use a minus-exposure compensation when taking photos of subjects that are quite dark in tone.

Problem	Solution
The corners of the image are dark	Remove any filter you have placed on a wide angle lens and replace with a slim-ring filter. Never use more than one filter at a time. (Mild darkening of the corners is common with many zoom lenses but should not be visible if shooting at f/8 or a smaller aperture.)
The images are blurry	This is often caused by camera shake or the movement of a subject. Make sure the Super SteadyShot button is set to On or mount the camera on a tripod. Set a higher ISO level for a faster shutter speed, particularly if the subject is moving.
An error message appears when trying to set custom White Balance	De-activate flash. If you do want to set Custom WB for flash, activate flash but move farther away from the white target being used to calibrate the system.
The camera will not play back images	Make sure the LCD display is on; press the DISP button. If the camera is hooked to a computer with a USB cable, disconnect it. If a file folder name has been changed in your computer, images can no longer be displayed on the camera. Also, images made with another camera cannot be displayed.

Before taking the A200 on a long trip where you will shoot many pho- ⇨
tos, it's worth becoming fully familiar with all of its features and the
problem-solving tips provided in this chapter.

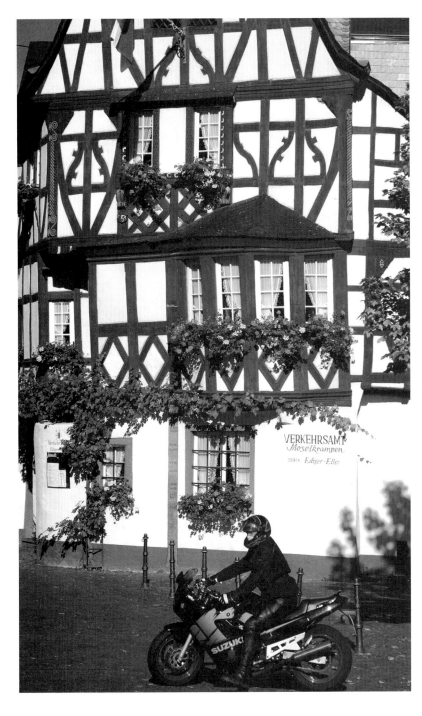

Glossary

aberration
An optical flaw in a lens that causes the image to be distorted or unclear.

Adobe Photoshop
Professional-level image-processing software with extremely powerful filter and color-correction tools.

Adobe Photoshop Elements
Elements lacks some of the more sophisticated controls available in Photoshop, but it does have a comprehensive range of image-manipulation options.

AF
See automatic focus.

ambient light
See available light.

anti-aliasing
A technique that reduces or eliminates the jagged appearance of lines or edges in an image.

aperture
The opening in the lens that allows light to enter the camera. Aperture is usually described as an f/number. The higher the f/number, the smaller the aperture; and the lower the f/number, the larger the aperture.

Aperture Priority mode
A semi-automatic operating mode in which you manually select the aperture and the camera automatically sets an appropriate shutter speed.

artifact
Information that is not part of the scene but appears in the image due to technology.

artificial light
Usually refers to any light source that doesn't exist in nature, such as incandescent, fluorescent, and other manufactured lighting.

automatic exposure
When the camera measures light and makes the adjustments necessary to create proper image density on sensitized media.

automatic flash
An electronic flash unit that reads light reflected off a subject (from either a pre-flash or the actual flash exposure), then shuts itself off as soon as ample light has reached the sensitized medium.

automatic focus
When the camera automatically adjusts the lens elements to sharply render the subject.

available light
The amount of illumination at a given location that applies to natural and artificial light sources but not those supplied specifically for photography. It is also called existing light or ambient light.

backlight
Light that projects toward the camera from behind the subject.

backup
A copy of a file or program. If the original is lost or damaged, the backup is still intact.

barrel distortion
A defect in the lens that makes straight lines curve outward away from the middle of the image.

bit
Binary digit. This is the basic unit of binary computation.

bit depth
The number of bits per pixel that determines the number of colors the image can display. Eight bits per pixel is the minimum requirement for a photo-quality color image.

bracketing
A sequence of pictures taken of the same subject but varying exposure, white balance or some other aspect, manually or automatically, between each image.

brightness
A subjective measure of illumination. See also, luminance.

buffer
A temporary data storage bank; in a camera, this bank stores image data before it is written to the memory card so the camera can continue taking images while data is still being recorded to the card.

built-in flash
A flash that is permanently attached to the camera body.

Bulb
A camera setting that allows the shutter to stay open as long as the shutter release is depressed.

card reader
A device that connects to your computer and enables quick and easy download of images from memory card to computer.

chromatic aberration
Occurs when light rays of different colors are focused on different planes, causing colored

halos around objects in the image.

chrominance
A component of an image that expresses the color (hue and saturation) information, as opposed to the luminance (lightness) values.

chrominance noise
A form of artifact that appears as a random scattering of densely packed colored "grain." See also, luminance and noise.

close-up
A general term used to describe an image created by closely focusing on a subject. Often involves the use of special lenses or extension tubes. Also, an automated exposure setting that automatically selects a large aperture (not available with all cameras).

color balance
The average overall color in a reproduced image. How a digital camera interprets the color of light in a scene so that white appears white while neutral gray appears neutral.

color cast
A colored hue over the image often caused by improper lighting or incorrect white balance settings. Can be produced intentionally for creative effect.

color space
A mapped relationship between colors and computer data about the colors.

CompactFlash (CF) card
One of the most widely used removable memory cards.

compression
A method of reducing file size, often through removal of "redundant" data, as with the JPEG file format.

contrast
The difference between two or more tones in terms of luminance, density, or darkness.

critical focus
The most sharply focused plane within an image.

cropping
The process of extracting a portion of the image area. If this portion of the image is enlarged, resolution is subsequently lowered.

dedicated flash
An electronic flash unit that communicates with the camera, passing on data such as flash illumination, lens focal length, subject distance, and sometimes flash status.

default

Refers to various factory-set functions; these can generally be changed by the user and re-set to the original factory settings.

depth of field

The image space in front of and behind the plane of focus that appears acceptably sharp in the image.

diopter

A measurement of the refractive power of a lens. Also, it may be a supplementary lens that is defined by its focal length and power of magnification.

download

The transfer of data from one device to another, such as from camera to computer or computer to printer.

dpi

Dots per inch. Used to define the resolution of a printer, this term refers to the number of dots of ink that a printer can lay down in an inch.

DPOF

Digital Print Order Format. A feature that enables the camera to supply data about the printing of image files and supplementary information contained within them. The printer must be DPOF compatible for the system to operate.

electronic flash

A device with a glass or plastic tube filled with gas that, when electrified, creates an intense flash of light. Also called a strobe. Unlike a flash bulb, it is reusable.

EV

Exposure value. A number that quantifies the amount of light within an scene, allowing you to determine the relative combinations of aperture and shutter speed to accurately reproduce the light levels of that exposure.

EXIF

Exchangeable Image File Format. This format is used for storing an image file's data or interchange information.

exposure

When light enters the camera and reacts with the sensitized medium. The term can also refer to the amount of light that strikes the light sensitive medium.

exposure meter

See light meter.

extension tube

A hollow metal ring that can be fitted between the camera and lens. It increases the distance between the optical center of the lens and the sensor and decreases the minimum focus distance of the lens.

f/

See f/stop

file format

The form in which digital images are stored and recorded, e.g., JPEG, ARW, TIFF, etc.

filter

Usually a piece of plastic or glass used to control how certain wavelengths of light are recorded. A filter absorbs selected wavelengths, preventing them from reaching the light sensitive medium. Also, software available in image-processing computer programs can produce special filter effects.

FireWire

A high speed data transfer standard that allows outlying accessories to be plugged and unplugged from the computer while it is turned on. Some digital cameras and card readers use FireWire to connect to a computer with a FireWire port. FireWire 400 (IEEE 1394a), FireWire 800 (IEEE 1394b) and FireWire S800T (IEEE 1394c) are available, all capable of faster data transfer than USB 2.0 Hi-Speed.

firmware

Software that is permanently incorporated into a hardware chip. All computer-based equipment, including digital cameras, use firmware of some kind.

flare
Unwanted light streaks or rings that appear in the viewfinder, on the recorded image, or both. It is caused by extrane-ous light striking the lens elements during shoot-ing. Use of a lens hood can often reduce this undesirable effect.

f/number
See f/stop.

focal length
When the lens is focused on infinity, it is the dis-tance from the optical center of the lens to the focal plane.

focal plane
The plane on which a lens forms a sharp image. This may be the film plane or sensor plane.

focus
An optimum sharpness or image clarity that occurs when a lens cre-ates a sharp image by converging light rays to specific points at the focal plane. The word also refers to the act of adjusting the lens to achieve optimal image sharpness.

f/stop
The size of the aperture or diaphragm opening of a lens, also referred to as f/number or stop. The term stands for the ratio

of the focal length (f) of the lens to the width of its aperture opening. (f/1.4 = wide opening and f/22 = narrow open-ing.) Each stop up (lower f/number) doubles the amount of light reaching the sensitized medium. Each stop down (higher f/number) halves the amount of light reaching the sensitized medium.

full-frame sensor
A sensor in a digital cam-era that has the same dimensions as a 35mm film frame (24 x 36 mm). Most DSLR cameras use a smaller sensor size.

GB
See gigabyte.

gigabyte
Just over one billion bytes.

GN
See guide number.

gray scale
A successive series of tones ranging between black and white, which have no color.

guide number
A number used to quan-tify the output of a flash unit. It is derived by using this formula: GN = aperture x distance. Guide numbers are expressed for a given ISO in either feet or meters.

hard drive
A contained storage unit made up of magnetically sensitive disks.

high-speed sync
Available with certain Sony and Maxxum/Dynax flash units, this feature allows the flash to be synchronized at shutter speeds up to 1/4000 second, instead of the usual maximum of 1/160 sec.

histogram
A graphic representation of image tones.

hot shoe
An electronically con-nected flash mount on the camera body. It enables direct connec-tion between the camera and an external flash, and synchronizes the shutter release with the firing of the flash.

image-editing or image-processing program
Software that allows for image alteration and enhancement.

infinity
In photographic terms, the theoretical most dis-tant point of focus.

interpolation
Process used to increase image resolution by creating new pixels based on existing pixels. The software intelligently looks at existing pixels and creates new pixels to fill the gaps and achieve a higher resolution.

IS
Image Stabilization. This is a technology that reduces camera shake and vibration. With some SLR systems, the mechanism is found in lenses. Sony's Super SteadyShot (SSS) system is inside the camera body.

ISO
A term for industry standards from the International Organization for Standardization. When an ISO number is applied to film, it indicates the relative light sensitivity of the recording medium. Digital sensors use film ISO equivalents, which are based on enhancing the data stream or boosting the signal with analog gain.

JPEG
Joint Photographic Experts Group. This is a lossy compression file format that works with any computer and photo software. JPEG examines an image for redundant information and then removes it. At low compression/high quality, the

loss of data has a negligible effect on the photo. However, JPEG should not be used as a working format—the file should be reopened and saved in a format such as TIFF, which does not compress the image.

LCD
Liquid Crystal Display, which is a flat screen with two clear polarizing sheets on either side of a liquid crystal solution. When activated by an electric current, the LCD causes the crystals to either pass through or block light in order to create a colored image display.

lens
A tube containing several pieces of optical glass in a formula that has been precisely calibrated to allow focus.

lens hood
Also called a lens shade. This is a short tube that can be attached to the front of a lens to reduce flare. It keeps undesirable light from reaching the front of the lens and also protects the front of the lens.

lens shade
See lens hood.

light meter
A device that measures light levels and calculates the correct aperture and shutter speed.

lithium-ion
A popular battery technology that is not prone to the charge memory effects of nickel-cadmium batteries, or the low temperature performance problems of alkaline batteries.

lossless
Image compression in which no data is lost. (The in-camera compression method used on RAW format files is lossless.)

lossy
Image compression in which data is lost and, thereby, image quality is lessened. (JPEG compression is lossy.) This means that the greater the compression, the lesser the image quality.

low-pass filter
A filter designed to remove elements of an image that correspond to high-frequency data, such as sharp edges and fine detail, to reduce the effect of moiré. See also, moiré.

luminance
A term used to describe directional brightness. It can also be used as luminance noise, which is a form of noise that appears as a sprinkling of black "grain."

M
See Manual exposure mode.

macro lens
A lens designed to be at top sharpness over a flat field when focused at close distances and reproduction ratios up to 1:1.

Manual mode
A camera operating mode that requires the user to determine and set both the aperture and shutter speed. This is the opposite of automatic exposure.

MB
See megabyte.

megabyte
Just over one million bytes.

megapixel
A million pixels.

memory
The storage capacity of a hard drive or other recording media.

memory card
A solid state removable storage medium that can store still images, moving images, or sound, as well as related file data. There are several different types including CompactFlash and various versions of Sony's Memory Stick.

menu
A listing of features, functions, or options dis-

played on a screen that can be selected and activated by the user.

Microdrive
A removable storage medium with moving parts. They are miniature hard drives based on the dimensions of a CompactFlash Type II card. Microdrives are more susceptible to the effects of impact, high altitude, and low temperature than solid-state cards are. See also, memory card.

middle gray
Halfway between black and white, it is an average gray tone with 18% reflectance. See also, gray card.

mid-tone
The tone that appears as medium brightness, or medium gray tone, in a photographic print.

moiré
Occurs when the subject has more detail than the resolution of the digital camera can capture. Moiré appears as a wavy pattern over the image.

noise
The digital equivalent of grain. It is often caused by a number of different factors, such as a high ISO setting, heat, sensor design, etc. and appears as a grainy effect, with mottled color specs. Though usually undesir-

able, it may be added for creative effect using an image-processing program. See also, chrominance noise and luminance.

normal lens
See standard lens.

overexposed
When too much light is recorded with the image, causing the photo to be too light in tone.

pan
Moving the camera to follow a moving subject. When a slow shutter speed is used, this creates an image in which the subject appears sharp and the background is blurred.

perspective
The effect of the distance between the camera and image elements upon the perceived size of objects in an image. It is also an expression of this three-dimensional relationship in two dimensions.

pincushion distortion
A flaw in a lens that causes straight lines to bend inward toward the middle of an image.

pixel
The base component of a digital image. Every individual pixel can have a distinct color and tone.

plug-in
Software, often created by third-parties, that can be added to an existing software program to provide additional features.

polarization
An effect achieved by using a polarizing filter. It minimizes reflections from non-metallic surfaces like water and glass and saturates colors by removing glare. Polarization often makes skies appear bluer at 90 degrees to the sun. The term also applies to the above effects simulated by a polarizing software filter.

pre-flashes
A series of short duration, low intensity flash pulses emitted by a flash unit immediately prior to the shutter opening. These flashes help the TTL light meter assess the reflectivity of the subject or when higher intensity of pre-flash is used, to minimize red-eye. See also, TTL.

Program mode
In this exposure mode, the camera selects a combination of shutter speed and aperture automatically but allows the user to select different combinations, while maintaining the same exposure.

RAW
An image file format that has little or no internal processing applied by the camera. It contains 12-bit color information, a wider range of data than 8-bit formats such as JPEG.

RAW+JPEG
An image file format that records two files per capture; one RAW file and one JPEG file.

rear curtain sync
A feature that causes the flash unit to fire just prior to the shutter closing. It is used for creative effect when mixing flash and ambient light.

red-eye reduction
A feature that causes the flash to emit a brief pulse of light just before the main flash fires. This helps to reduce the effect of retinal reflection.

resolution
The amount of data available for an image as applied to image size. It is expressed in pixels or megapixels, or sometimes as lines per inch on a monitor or dots per inch on a printed image.

RGB mode
Red, Green, and Blue. This is the color model most commonly used to display color images on video systems, film recorders, and computer monitors. It displays all visible colors as combinations of red, green, and blue. RGB mode is the most common color mode for viewing and working with digital files onscreen and for image capture in a digital camera.

saturation
The degree to which a color of fixed tone varies from the neutral, grey tone; low saturation produces pastel shades whereas high saturation gives deep, bold, vivid color.

sharp
A term used to describe the quality of an image as clear, crisp, and perfectly focused, as opposed to fuzzy, obscure, or unfocused.

shutter
The apparatus that controls the amount of time during which light is allowed to reach the sensitized medium.

Shutter Priority mode
A semi-automatic exposure mode in which you manually select the shutter speed and the camera automatically selects an appropriate aperture size or f/stop.

Single-lens reflex
See SLR.

slow sync
A flash mode in which a slow shutter speed is used with the flash in order to allow low-level ambient light to be recorded by the sensitized medium.

SLR
Single-lens reflex. A camera with a mirror that reflects the image entering the lens through a pentaprism or pentamirror onto the viewfinder screen. When you take the picture, the mirror reflexes out of the way, the focal plane shutter opens, and the image is recorded.

standard lens
Also known as a normal lens, this is a fixed-focal-length lens usually in the range of 45 to 55mm for 35mm format or approximately 35mm in a digital camera with a sensor that is smaller than a 35mm film frame. In contrast to wide-angle or telephoto lenses, a standard lens views a realistically proportionate perspective of a scene.

stop down
To reduce the size of the diaphragm opening by using a higher f/number (smaller aperture).

stop up
To increase the size of the diaphragm opening by using a lower f/number (wider aperture).

synchronize
Causing a flash unit to fire simultaneously with the complete opening of the camera's shutter; with the ·200, the fastest "sync speed" is 1/160 sec.

telephoto lens
A lens with a long focal length that enlarges the subject and produces a narrower angle of view than you would see with your eyes.

thumbnail
A small representation of an image file used principally for identification purposes.

TIFF
Tagged Image File Format. This popular digital format can be compressed in a computer, using lossless compression.

tripod
A three-legged stand that stabilizes the camera and eliminates camera shake caused by body movement or vibration. Tripods are usually adjustable for height and angle.

TTL
Through-the-Lens, i.e. TTL metering.

USB
Universal Serial Bus. This interface standard allows outlying accessories to be plugged and unplugged from the computer while it is turned on. USB 2.0 is faster than previous USB versions but USB 2.0 Hi-speed is required for the fastest data transfer possible with USB. (The ·200 is USB 2.0 compliant.)

vignetting
An obvious darkening at the edges of an image (duet to a reduction of light) caused by an inappropriate lens hood for the particular lens or the use of a very thick filter.

viewfinder or viewing screen
The ground glass surface in an SLR camera's viewfinder, on which you view your image

wide-angle lens
A lens that produces a greater angle of view than you would see with your eyes, often causing the image to appear stretched. See also, short lens.

Wireless Flash
A system that allows for off-camera flash using an accessory flash unit that is triggered by a burst of light from the camera's built-in flash.

zoom lens
A lens that can be adjusted to cover a wide range of focal lengths.

219

Index